1994

CLINTONCARE

CLINTONCARE

PUTTING
GOVERNMENT
IN CHARGE OF
YOUR HEALTH

DR. BARRY ASMUS

AMERIPRESS

Phoenix, Arizona

ISBN: 0-9640421-0-X

COVER DESIGN: James Cowlin
BOOK DESIGN: Alan Korwin

ATTENTION clubs, organizations, educators and all interested parties: Ask the publisher about quantity discounts!
(602) 953-5149.

Printed and bound in the United States of America

10 9 8 7 6 5 4 3 2 1

Acknowledgements

I am immeasurably indebted to Donald B. Billings for his excellent research and assistance in the preparation of this book. In his own right Don is a gifted economist and writer. As a friend and professional colleague, his tireless work made this book a reality.

Also, to David Henderson, Senior Research Fellow at Stanford University's Hoover Institute, who read and improved the entire manuscript and to Merrill Mathews of the National Center for Policy Analysis, for help in editing, my deepest thanks. Allen Dalton, a former colleague and Director of the Center for the Study of Market Alternatives, also read the manuscript and provided helpful comments.

v

Dedication

To the 562 economists who warned the President in a January 14, 1994 *Wall Street Journal* article of the terrible consequences of the Clinton health care plan.

They concluded that, "patients will face delays of months and years for surgery, government bureaucrats will decide treatment options instead of doctors and patients, and innovations in medical techniques and pharmaceuticals will be dramatically reduced."

The plan would produce "lower quality medical care, reduced medical innovation, and expensive new bureaucracies. These controls will hurt people and will damage the economy."

Table of Contents

CHAPTER ONE

Introduction

President Clinton and Hillary Rodham Clinton, with the help of advisers Ira Magaziner, Paul Starr, and Walter Zelman, have asked Congress to adopt a massive bureaucratic plan that could destroy the finest health care system in the world. The President claims that ClintonCare is based on "security, simplicity, savings, choice, quality, and health care that's always there." In

---

The Clinton planners say our system is too complicated and expensive. But they propose the most complicated and expensive piece of legislation imaginable.

---

fact, it is a scheme that is about neither health nor security, and it is definitely not simple. It is about asserting government power and limiting personal choice. In page after mind-numbing page the plan threatens consumers, limits the ways health care suppliers can compete and practice medicine, slows medical innovation, rejects the use of market incentives,

and raises taxes to boot. The Clinton planners say our
system is too complicated and expensive. But they
propose the most complicated and expensive piece of
legislation imaginable.

ClintonCare would be bad for America. It would
require everyone to have the same benefits package, and
the federal government would decide what benefits to
include. For example, women over the age of 50 would
be eligible for a free mammogram, while women under
50 would not. A child's vaccination for whooping cough
would be free; a flu shot would not.

ClintonCare would mean fewer choices for patients
about where and from whom they receive their care.
Criminal penalties would be imposed if we seek
alternative coverage, or less coverage, for that matter,
than the government's plan would offer. The plan's
provisions would place the current option of fee-for-
service, private practice at a big disadvantage. It would
force most people into managed care, HMO-type
provider organizations where they would no longer have
the right to make their own health care decisions. That
privilege would fall to the managed care group to which
one belonged.

The Clinton plan would create many new
government bureaucracies, and regulations would
proliferate. A National Health Board, with members
appointed by the President, would establish a global
budget for health care spending, mandate regulations it
deemed necessary, and impose sanctions on individuals,
businesses and states that failed to comply. Many other
new bureaucracies would be created, including a
National Council on Graduate Medical Education and
ten regional councils that would control the number of
physicians allowed to practice and in what specialities.

Since medical care would more than ever be
perceived as being "free," demand would grow and a real
problem, escalating health costs, would not be brought
under control. If you believe health care is expensive
now, just wait until you see what it costs when the
Clintons make it free. Rationing of health care would

follow, as it has in Canada, New Zealand, and Britain. Inevitably, the quality of medical care would suffer.

We are asked to believe that a government mandate would make our employer pay most of the bill. In fact, a massive new federal payroll tax—the Clintons call it a mandated employer and employee "premium"—would increase hiring costs and destroy jobs. In sum, the

---

A National Health Board, with members appointed by the President, would establish a global budget for health care spending, mandate regulations it deemed necessary, and impose sanctions on individuals, businesses and states that failed to comply

---

Clinton administration threatens to violate Hippocrates (c. 460–c. 377 B.C.) first rule of the physician's oath: Do No Harm!

Why do the Clintons believe that command-and-control economics would work for one-seventh of the American economy when it didn't work in the old Soviet Union, or for that matter, anywhere else? Government-controlled, socialist economies have failed wherever they have been tried.

Could the Clintons' pursuit of bureaucratic solutions result from their ideological bias? As with most intellectuals and political types, the Clintons do seem to favor political and therefore bureaucratic solutions over the market economy. The President and Mrs. Clinton, and their principle health care advisers, apparently do not understand or appreciate the benefits of free-market solutions to economic problems. The fact is that incentives matter. Rewards and penalties influence choices.

Actually, political strategy seems the most plausible explanation of ClintonCare. They have followed the strategic advice of Clinton's pollster Stanley Greenberg.

Following George Bush's victory in 1988, which meant three consecutive terms in the White House for the Republicans, Greenberg advocated a new liberal strategy for the 1992 Presidential election.[1]   If the Democrats were going to win back the "Reagan Democrats" and therefore the White House, they would have to create a new government goodie for the middle-class. When Mr. Clinton's "stimulus" spending package

---

Market-oriented reforms would increase patient choice, increase competition, control health care costs, and maintain access to the finest health care system in the world.

---

for "investment" failed to pass Congress early in 1993, *The Wall Street Journal* reported that the President confided to aids that the "only thing we'll really have to give the American people is health care." [2]

But bigger government requires more money. Even taxing the rich has its limits. Large increases in government revenues would have to come from the middle class. The goal of the Greenberg/Clinton strategy would be to establish another broad-based "entitlement" (a "right") that would make a large majority of Americans more dependent on government handouts. According to Greenberg, "Democrats need to rediscover broad-based social policy that sends a larger message: Democrats are for everybody, not just the have-nots." The middle class would join ethnic minorities and other so-called disadvantaged groups to form a working political majority for the Democratic party.

Additional taxes, we were told, would not be required. It would seemingly be "free." Employers would buy our health care for us. Unfortunately for working men and women, free and expanded health care benefits would translate into lower wages, salaries and other benefits as well as higher taxes. In exchange for the promise of "security," Americans would sacrifice their freedom.

The political and bureaucratic solutions offered by ClintonCare are counterproductive. A preferred solution to the problems in our health care system requires market-oriented reforms that would increase patient choice, increase competition, control health care costs, and maintain access to the finest health care system in the world.

CHAPTER TWO

The Clinton Plan

Instead of moving toward genuine, competitive markets for health care services, the Clintons offer a grand, political scheme. Building on a government bureaucracy whose consequences are unknown, they conveniently ignore the predictable drawbacks of centrally planned, political solutions. In their deliberations, Hillary Rodham Clinton and her group of 500 health-care "experts" rejected market-oriented and actuarially-sound health insurance. Instead they opted for "managed competition," with a resounding emphasis on *managed*. They missed the opportunity to modify the federal tax code, and therefore rid the existing system of major impediments to market reform. They failed to consider empowering individual consumers with vouchers, medical savings accounts or tax credits to encourage careful spending. And they also ignored market-oriented reforms to tort liability in the legal system. Instead they opted for a massive extension of the welfare state.

Hillary's Health Care Task Force Operated In Secret

Apparently because of what *The Wall Street Journal* calls "Mrs. Clinton's Czarist Past" and her work as head of Governor Bill Clinton's education commission in Arkansas, Hillary Rodham Clinton was given command of the secretive Health Care Task Force. Ira Magaziner, who is famous for advocating national economic planning, directed the group on a day-by-day basis. The work of this odd assortment of federal bureaucrats and academic social engineers—and noticeably without wide-spread representation from the health care industries—was really more subterfuge than

The Clintons want to micro-manage a major part of the economy—America's health care— even though they couldn't organize the task force charged with planning it.

substance. ClintonCare, the plan to politicize and bureaucratize American health care, had already been hatched before the Presidential election .[3]

The radical plan was largely built on Magaziner's arrogant and unrealistic conviction that "universal" and mostly "free" health care coverage could be financed by "recapturing" savings and "squeezing" waste out of the existing system. In contrast to the expectations of most outside experts, then and now, this would supposedly be accomplished, according to the Clinton planners, by creating *more* government bureaucracy, not less.

The disorganization that characterized the group's deliberations suggests the inefficiencies to be expected from a government-managed health care system. A federal judge requested documents pertaining to the health care task force's work in order to rule on the legality of the secrecy being maintained by the group.

The task force responded that deliberations were disorganized. Complete records had not been kept.

The proposed National Health Board would have unprecedented power to impose rules and regulations, to establish spending ceilings on health care, and to determine benefits.

In other words, the Clintons want to micro-manage America's health care, a major part of the economy, even though they were unable to organize the task force charged with planning it. Humorist P. J. O'Rourke captured the essence of what we were denied: "We are not allowed to watch Hillary's 'Gang of 500' presumably for the same reason we shouldn't watch the manufacture of sausage."[4]

Soviet Planning in America: The Health Care Security Act

Mrs. Clinton, Magaziner, Paul Starr and Walter Zelman have picked and combined elements from many health care reform schemes, always choosing the path of more government control and bureaucracy in lieu of market solutions. Like Dr. Frankenstein, they have ended up with a monster. Merrill Mathews and Molly Hering have captured the scope and flavor of the bureaucratic beast:

It won't be Bill or Hillary Clinton who will tell you that you can't have a brain scan. You're going to be told that by a bureaucrat who reports to a large HMO bureaucracy, which reports to an alliance bureaucracy, which reports to a state-government bureaucracy, which reports to a National Health Board bureaucracy, whose chief just happens to have been appointed by the President.[5]

The leading players in the tragic drama would be "managed care" health care providers, such as Health Maintenance Organizations (HMOs) and Preferred Provider Organizations (PPOs), large bureaucratic purchasing cooperatives called health alliances, and state health bureaucracies. All, in turn, would be controlled by the new National Health Board.

The proposed National Health Board would have unprecedented power to impose rules and regulations, to establish spending ceilings on health care, and to determine benefits. It would also have the police power to impose penalties and sanctions on states, health alliances, health care providers, and even individuals for violating the mass of bureaucratic rules embodied in their initial 1,342-page legislative package. Thousands of additional pages would also be necessary to spell out how the bureaucracy would implement and control the draconian mandates and regulations required by ClintonCare.

The Board's power is suggested by the authoritarian language that appears throughout the proposal. For example: "The National Health Board may promulgate such regulations as may be necessary," and, "The board shall have authority... to appoint such officers and employees as are necessary to carry out its functions."[6]

The political and therefore bureaucratic character of the plan would be reinforced by the following new bureaucracies, among others: the Advisory Council on Breakthrough Drugs, the National Long Term Care Insurance Advisory Council, the National Council Regarding Workforce Priorities, the National Council on Graduate Medical Education, the National Institute for Health Care Workforce Development, the National Quality Management Council, the National Quality Consortium, the National Privacy and Health Data Advisory Council, the Federal Health Plan Review Board and the Advisory Commission on Regional Variations in Health Expenditures. The administration's 239-page preliminary draft in

September 1993 revealed that the Clinton plan would create 59 new federal programs or bureaucracies, expand 20 others, and impose 79 new federal mandates.[7] The Clintons, in turn, maintain the outrageous view that this enormous expansion of government control will be part of a process which *reduces* paperwork.   Have they left their earthly moorings?

Hillary Rodham Clinton and Ira Magaziner talk a great deal about expanded personal choice, but that is *not* the way the new bureaucratic system would work.

The Clintons maintain the outrageous view that this enormous expansion of government control will reduce paperwork.

The list of criminal and civil penalties in their plan lays to rest the oft-repeated claims that ClintonCare is based on choice and market incentives. They have announced that one plan fits all. And the power to make us play seems assured. The Supreme Court's sorry record since the 1930s in defending our economic freedoms, including the right of contract, suggests that the Clinton health plan or one like it would probably be upheld in the federal courts.   A mandated single-plan-for-all government health care system would be the end of Constitutional restraint. David Rivkin of the American Enterprise Institute summarizes the stark implications:

> [We] will be dragooned into the system for no other reason than that [we] are people who are here. If the courts uphold Congress's authority to impose this system, they must once and for all draw the curtain on the Constitution of 1787 and admit that there is *nothing* that Congress cannot do under the Commerce Clause. The polite fiction that we live

under a government of limited powers must be discarded—Leviathan must be embraced.[8]

Managed Competition is the Ultimate Oxymoron

The center piece of the Clinton health care reform package is "managed competition." Each state would be required to establish one or more health alliances (i.e. purchasing alliances or purchasing cooperatives) to which all Americans, except the employees of companies with more than 5,000 employees, must belong. Usually there would be just one alliance in an area. Health alliances, using market buying power, would purchase the benefit package on behalf of their business and individual members.

Qualified managed care providers, such as HMOs and PPOs, would competitively bid to supply the government-defined medical benefits package to a large purchasing alliance. Individuals and families, through their employers, would be required to choose one of the managed care providers in their alliance area to supply their medical care. The health alliances would report to state governments and ultimately to the newly created federal National Health Board. In the October 1993 edition of the Clinton plan, individual states would find it relatively easy to create state-wide, single-payer plans such as the government-run health care system in Canada. Interestingly, in 1993 the Canadian government began a drastic cost-cutting program in their system which is leading to even more rationing of health care.

In spite of the stifling bureaucratic control offered by the Clinton plan, the administration claims that it recognizes the advantages of a market economy. ClintonCare would retain private ownership of hospitals and other managed care organizations, instead of outright government operation. But, fee-for-service medicine, as currently practiced, would, for all practical purposes, be eliminated, reducing the choices available to consumers. And many of the best doctors would choose to leave medicine rather than be forced to work, in effect, for government.

If President Clinton and Hillary Rodham Clinton really believe that the way to control health care costs is to "manage" the free and open market process, we are in deep trouble. Architects of the original idea of managed competition, economist Alain Enthoven and physician Paul Ellwood, both of the Jackson Hole group, have explicitly rejected the Clinton plan. Enthoven has stated that the administration is "redefining the concept" of a health alliance, and that it "threatens to be a monopolistic, regulatory government agency that will cause more problems than it solves."[9] He continues: "The first thing Congress should do is delete pages one through 1,342 of Clinton's 1,342-page bill."

In summary, managed competition is a euphemism for government control. Paul Starr of Princeton University, an influential member of Hillary's "Gang of 500," seeks to avoid any misunderstanding: "The surest way to kill managed competition," according to Starr, "is to make the purchasing cooperatives voluntary." Walter Zelman, a California health-issues expert and member of the advisory group, stated that the health care purchasing alliances should be an "arm of government."[10]

In summary, managed competition is a euphemism for government control.

The Clintons' political proposal to solve America's health care "crisis" sounds and reads very much like what the Italian Fascist's in the 1930s called "corporatism." According to Fausto Pitigliani, a supporter of Mussolini, "The Italian National Council of Corporations" (Read: National Health Board) was to regulate Italian industry "in a manner concordant with the interests of the national economy" and to create a "spirit of national collaboration."[11]   Italy's experiment with Fascism and government control over private enterprise failed, as do most government-divined interventions in the free-market economy. Bureaucratic government control over private industry through mandates and regulations has never delivered the promised goods.

If It Looks Like A Tax And Acts Like A Tax Then It Is A Tax

The Clinton plan proposes to finance universal and seemingly free health care for all Americans by mandating that businesses pay 80 percent of their employees' health "insurance premium." The employee would, in turn, pay 20 percent. In the beginning, large companies would have a maximum responsibility equal to 7.9 percent of their payroll. Small businesses with fewer than 75 employees and paying relatively low wages would receive a sliding scale subsidy. Firms with the lowest wages would pay no more than 3.5 percent of their payroll.

By blatantly calling their huge tax increase a mandated premium payment instead of a payroll tax, the administration seeks to hide the cost of this radical plan from the American people.

Individuals, in turn, would be required to pay no more than 3.9 percent of their earnings toward the cost of their health care. For example, if the average cost for a family, determined by the projected outlays and required revenues, equaled $4,500 a year, the family would be directly responsible for twenty percent, or $900. If the family's income were less than $23,077

($900 equals 3.9% of $23,077), they would receive a government subsidy.

Unfortunately, many people believe their employer will *really* pay 80 percent of the cost of their health insurance. That is false. Economists are nearly unanimous in the view that eventually the employee bears the full burden of the payroll tax. Whether in the form of lower wages, reductions in other employee benefits, or even by losing their jobs, employees pay for "employer" mandates.

The costs of labor to a business include all forms of compensation. To remain competitive, particularly in the new global economy, a company must absorb a new payroll tax within the constraints imposed by its overall costs and sales. In other words, shifting the employer mandate to business owners and/or consumers would be very difficult.

Employees will, in the end, pay the full amount of the tax imposed to finance their health care. There is no such thing as a free lunch. There are cheap lunches though. Under the Clinton plan, those who won't work or who practice unhealthy life styles would be subsidized at the expense of others.

Blatantly calling their huge tax increase a mandated premium payment instead of a payroll tax, the administration also seeks to hide the cost of this radical plan from the American people. As 1994 began, and as the Clintons contemplate having the government take over a large part of the U.S. economy, they have been campaigning to keep health care spending and the taxes necessary to finance these outlays out of the regular federal budget.

Proposing Radical Surgery Has Turned Economics On Its Head

The administration has tried to convince us that the health care system is broken and requires a complete, government-led overhaul. Claiming that thirty-seven million people are uninsured, the Clintons prescribe radical surgery. Yet, a closer look at this number reveals that being uninsured does *not* mean you cannot get health care or that most people are without insurance for long periods of time. What it really means is that uninsured people are more likely to rely on emergency-room care rather than office care or on the billions of dollars of free care that many physicians provide each year.

The Pioneer Institute for Public Policy, a Boston research firm, tells us that almost three-fifths of the 37 million uninsured are young adults under the age of 30

Eventually, the employees bear the full burden of the payroll tax—in lower wages, reductions in benefits, and even lost jobs.

---

who don't feel a need for insurance, at least at current inflated prices. Half of the uninsured go without coverage for less than 5 months and 70 percent for less than 12 months. The vast majority of uninsured who are capable of working reacquire coverage within a year.

The administration also contends that Americans are spending too much on health care, that health care is a burden. But what they have really done is turn economic thinking on its head. As incomes have risen in recent decades, American families have increased their purchases of many goods and services faster than their incomes—new automobiles, leisure activities, restaurant dinning, as well as medical care. Today we are buying cellular phones, personal computers, and cruise vacations as though there is no tomorrow.

And the new technology embodied in these products—such as safer and more fuel efficient cars, rough-weather stabilizers on cruise ships, and miniaturized electronics—are thought highly desirable by consumers.

New technology increases the satisfaction that we get from the goods and services that contain superior quality. Compact disks are superior to cassettes which are preferred to long-play phonograph records.

Increased purchases of goods and services are almost always viewed as being a good thing, and rightly so. If people spend more on the things that, in their own view, improve their lives, we usually conclude that they are better off.

Health care, for the Clintons and their advisers, is somehow different. Mysteriously, we are told that increased spending on medical care is a burden rather than a benefit. Advances in medical technology, we are told, are likewise undesirable. According to this view, there is simply too much technology in health care. As a result, rather than viewing advanced technology as part of the solution, the Clintons would restrict access to technological breakthroughs. Third-party payers of medical bills, especially the Medicare and Medicaid programs and at least some private insurance companies, faced with perverse incentives, have become more and more hostile to the development of new technologies.

Something is horribly wrong with this topsy-turvy interpretation. Improved medical technology, although quite expensive to develop, invariably leads to faster and more accurate diagnoses and more cost-effective

---

Stopping progress solves nothing. The real problem is that free-market forces have not been permitted to operate in large parts of the health care sector.

---

care. We are not just spending more. We are getting more for our money, especially quality.

Many Americans have *chosen* to spend more of their income on health care just as they have chosen to spend more of their income on eating out. Having achieved the highest standard of living in the world, and having met other needs, it is natural that people will choose to spend more on protecting their health. We spend more on health care than the English, in part, because we are wealthier.

Stopping progress solves nothing. The real problem is that free-market forces have *not* been permitted to operate in large parts of the health care sector. Individuals receiving "free" medical care are not cost-conscious. Unless and until we empower individuals to buy their medical care with their own money in competitive markets, *less* technology will, unfortunately, continue to be viewed as progress.

A Case Study:
Political Bureaucracy In Action

Before turning to an orderly treatment of the undesirable consequences to be expected from the Clinton plan, I want to share with you the experiences of a family trying to deal with the existing federal bureaucracy. The story underlines what we can expect if ClintonCare becomes law and new bureaucracies work their inevitable ways.

The following article first appeared in *The Wall Street Journal*. It is the personal story of Marianne Jennings, a professor of legal and ethical studies at Arizona State University and a friend of many of us in the Phoenix area through her twice-a-week column in *The Arizona Republic*.[12]

A Mother Talks to Mrs. Clinton

My husband and I have the privilege of raising a child with severe mental and physical impairments. If you were to ask me the most difficult aspect of rearing this unique little girl, the answer would not be the countless hospitalizations, the equipment demands, the sleepless nights or the too-long stares when we're in public. It would be the government bureaucracies we face to provide for her, protect her and help her tap her potential.

As I listen to Hillary Rodham Clinton tout the wonders of a national health care plan, I want to say: "Come follow me, Mrs. Clinton. I can show you what government does to those it sets out to help."

I would begin by introducing Mrs. Clinton to the five or so caseworkers assigned to our Claire. One is from Arizona's Department of Development Disability. Another is with Arizona Long Term Care. Another is with the Arizona Health Care Cost Containment System. Another is with APIPA, and I don't know what that stands for. I lost track of acronyms, agencies and caseworkers long ago.

These caseworkers, assigned as advocates for my daughter's needs, come to our house, one by one, once each year to conduct two-hour interviews and verify in person that Claire, a child who is now six and has never spoken, has not been the recipient of a miracle cure.

I don't know what the caseworkers do beyond this interview but two things have occurred to me. First, burglars could just arrive at our door with a lot of forms and an acronym and anyone in the household would let them in. Second, there must be yet another contrived constitutional privacy right or some insider trading rule that prohibits state and federal employees who work with the same family from using one file, comparing notes, sharing information or even car pooling for interviews. My favorite interview was last fall, when a caseworker was assigned to redo hundreds of interviews as part of a new total-quality management program.

If I could introduce Mrs. Clinton to our five caseworkers, I would ask her to pose a hypothetical question to them about Claire's coverage. Mrs. Clinton would get five to eight different answers. The eight is because some of the caseworkers who buy into the new TQM program would go beyond the call of duty and give us two to three wrong possibilities.

I would then take Mrs. Clinton into the world of Title XIX, a federal benefits program administered by the state for children under 19 who have permanent disabilities. Theoretically, Title XIX means summer school, swimming programs, respite care, therapy and a host of services that make it sound like a luxury spa. Reality is quite another story.

Title XIX qualifies children on the basis of need (i.e. income) or degree of disability. Claire qualified on the basis of disability, but we are still required once each year to submit to an in-office interview (with yet another caseworker) in which I must give copies of our car titles, house deed, bank account statements, W2s and the like. A sample caseworker's comment from one year's interview: "I see you have a new piano in your home. Claire doesn't play this, does she?" I had to wonder why someone looking at a child who can't sit, hold her head up or make any discernible voluntary movements felt compelled to ask such a question.

One year we made the monumental mistake of adding Claire to our car title. Claire must be on the car title in Arizona for us to have a handicapped license plate. When we had only a movable permit that was placed in the front

---

I was required to sign a witnessed statement that said our cortically blind kindergartner did not take the Chevy Suburban out for spins.

---

window, people yelled at us in parking lots. With our official plates, we were saved from such grocery store skirmishes. But I had to face the glare of a Title XIXer who said, "Is Claire driving this car?" I was required to sign a witnessed statement that said our cortically blind kindergartner did not take the Chevrolet Suburban out for spins.

During our income interview last year, a caseworker spotted our medical expenses. They are our biggest expense even with insurance, exceeding our house payments and food costs each month. The caseworker asked, "Why would you pay medical bills?" I never know about trick questions in bureaucratic territory, so I responded, "Because we owe them?"

She then explained—the first government employee in four years to spot the issue—that Title XIX covered all of Claire's medical expenses not covered by another insurance. I asked, "How come no one ever told me this?" To which she responded, "because they didn't know."

Once you're in Title XIX, it is Disney's Space Mountain—dark and twisted. In 1992 I began asking for summer school approval in April. I received approval on July 22—three days before summer school ended. Last year I began the summer school approval quest in February. I got it in April, but someone forgot to put Claire's name on the registration list. I found this out after a two-hour wait in the registration line. I paid for summer school myself and have since learned the term "refund" is not part of Title XIX.

I began using our newly discovered Title XIX medical benefits in August. In just six weeks, I received authorization for a new wheelchair and a scoliosis jacket. In October I got a call from a caseworker who informed me that Claire's Title XIX benefits were being terminated as of that day.

I can show Mrs. Clinton that programs like hers already exist. I can show her the paperwork, the idiosyncratic rules, the insensitivity, the ill-trained workers and a bureaucracy as deep as the Mississippi at St. Louis. I can show her a system that, much like her proposal, was intended to help.

He had discovered on the forms that I fill out for the financial interview a $1,600 bank account for Claire. It was a burial account within the $1,500 limit allowed by statute, but it had earned interest. Claire had too much income. I offered to close the account. "Too late," he said. Then he added, "But you can always come down and reapply for Title XIX. It took me six months to get qualified the first time. I should have us reinstated just in time for summer school next year.

I am a lawyer who teaches and writes about administrative process. Yet this system is beyond my expertise. How do parents with language barriers, little or no knowledge of due process and non-compulsive personalities cope?

I can show Mrs. Clinton that programs like hers already exist. I can show her the paperwork, the idiosyncratic rules, the insensitivity, the ill-trained workers and a bureaucracy as deep as the Mississippi at St. Louis. I can show her a system that, much like her proposal, was intended to help. The reality is that help rarely makes it to our Claire.

CHAPTER THREE

Problems with the Clinton Plan

ClintonCare would be hard on your freedom, your health, and your pocketbook. The plan is badly flawed. There are eight important problems.

First, government is already heavily involved in America's health care, and the results, as with most government intervention in the market, are not encouraging. There is no reason to believe that government can control health care costs.

Second, the nationalized, government-controlled systems of "universal coverage" in Canada and Great Britain have failed to guarantee equal access to health care. ClintonCare would be no different.

Third, the Clinton plan would deny patient control over their health care choices. Not only would choosing one's own doctors be more difficult, but restrictions on choosing insurance coverage, such as benefit packages, deductibles, co-payments and stop-loss cutoffs, would be drastically curtailed, if not eliminated. The single benefits package leaves no room for individual preferences. *157, 902*

Fourth, the administration's "community rating" mandate of "premium" payments being the same for everyone in a health plan, irrespective of personal conduct, would create perverse incentives. Encouraging dangerous and unhealthy life-style choices would undoubtedly contribute to a further decline in social and moral standards that we see all around us.

Fifth, the Clinton plan fails to recognize the inevitable inefficiency and waste of treating health care as free when consumed. It's amazing how much of something people want when they do not have to pay. Health experts call this the third-party payment problem.

Sixth, the plan's "global budget," a ceiling on total health care spending, and other price controls would necessarily require more costly means of rationing health care.

Seventh, health care rationing would, in turn, inevitably cause a deterioration in the quality of American health care.

And, finally, the massive new payroll tax would increase labor costs, in particular the cost of hiring, and therefore destroy many thousands of jobs. These job losses are above and beyond those associated with the substitution of additional government bureaucracy for many private insurance companies and other provider organizations that would be forced out of the health insurance business. Let's look at the facts.

Government Is Already A Big Player In America's Health Care

The Clinton Health Security Act would, the Clintons say, guarantee universal and equal access to health care *and* simultaneously control the spiraling increase in health care costs. How is that possible? The federal bureaucracy already controls a significant part of the pricing and practice of American medicine, ostensibly to "control costs" as well as to insure the delivery of health care to certain groups. Total government health care outlays in 1992 represented about 45 percent of total U.S. health care spending, up from 24 percent in 1960. Medicare and Medicaid alone reached two-thirds of total government health outlays in 1992 or 30 percent of total U.S. health care spending, up from just 5.9 percent in 1967, the first full year of Medicare and Medicaid expenditures.

The massive new payroll tax would increase labor costs, in particular the cost of hiring, and therefore destroy many thousands of jobs.

The federal government's operation of Medicare, Medicaid and Veterans' hospitals provides evidence of government's inability to control costs. Government's early projections of growth in Medicare spending were spectacularly wrong. In the first year of the Medicare program, outlays were $3 billion. In 1965, the government projected Medicare spending of $9 billion for 1990. Actual spending in 1990: $98 billion! Explosive increases in spending have also been the story of Medicaid.[13]

The notion of "government cost control," perhaps the ultimate oxymoron, seems an absurd concept in

---

The inescapable conclusion is that the federal government has been a major force in driving costs higher over the past three decades.

---

light of the record. The inescapable conclusion is that the federal government has been a major force in driving health care costs higher over the past three decades.

Predictably, exploding Medicare and Medicaid budgets have led to price controls and health care rationing. In 1983, the federal government imposed a system of Medicare reimbursement based on what are called diagnosis-related groups (DRGs). These were essentially ceiling prices for almost 500 categories of hospital services. The system of price controls was later expanded to include physician reimbursements. Because the DRG prices are frequently lower than the market price for providing the service, both rationing and shifting costs to private insurers were inevitable. Private parties pay significantly more for their health insurance to cover the costs of the government programs. Rationing, as we will see, has a frightful potential for causing the quality of medical care to deteriorate.[14]

Socialism Doesn't Guarantee Equal Access

The centerpiece of the Clinton commitment to universal coverage is the goal of equal access for all Americans to quality health care. In 1948, equal access also dominated the thinking of Aneurin Bevan, the father of the National Health Service (NHS) in Great Britain: "The essence of a satisfactory health service is that rich and poor are treated alike, that poverty is not a disability and wealth is not advantaged."[15]

Rationing health care has a frightful potential for causing the quality of medical care to deteriorate.

But the overriding concern of Communism and socialism for equality has always failed to equalize access to health care. The story is the same in Britain, Canada and other politically-controlled health care systems. According to the Black Report, a 1980 study by the British government's Department of Health and Social Security, there was little evidence of more equal access to health care in Britain since the founding of the NHS in 1948. In 1987, this evidence was reaffirmed in an article appropriately entitled "Dying of Inequality."[16]

Other studies have documented similar results for New Zealand, Canada, and Sweden among other countries. And in each country the evidence suggests that the burden of unequal health care expenditures is borne by lower-income groups in small towns and rural areas. In British Columbia, Canada for example, disparities in access to treatment between some areas are startling. Per capita expenditures on the services of physician specialists in the city of Vancouver are three times as high as in the town of Peace River.[17]

When government takes charge of something, the results are always bureaucratic and therefore inefficient. An additional and inevitable outcome, reduced freedom, was starkly outlined by Enoch Powell, former Minister of Health who ran Britain's nationalized system:

> Whatever is entrusted to politicians becomes political even if it is not political anyhow....The phenomena of Medicine and Politics...result automatically and necessarily from the nationalization of medical care and its provision gratis at the point of consumption... These phenomena are implicit in such an organization and are not the accidental or incidental results of blemishes which can be 'reformed' away while leaving the system as such intact.[18]

The irony is that the U.S. has been doing a better job on access, especially of sophisticated, high-tech procedures for the seriously ill, than the national systems that our leaders seem to envy. Health care experts John C. Goodman and Gerald L. Musgrave in *Twenty Myths About National Health Insurance* offer a profound observation about access to health care:

"Considering the rationing of medical technology in countries with national health insurance, the United States may have gone further in removing barriers to medical care than any other country in the world."[19]

The American People Want To Choose Their Own Doctor

Contrary to claims by the administration, the Clinton plan would, if passed, force everyone into an HMO-style, managed care system. Price ceilings on the premiums that fee-for-service plans could charge would largely eliminate this alternative type of practice. In addition, low deductibles would be mandated. This would increase the premiums necessary for fee-for-service plans to stay in business.

The irony is that the U.S. has been doing a better job on access, especially of sophisticated, high-tech procedures for the seriously ill, than the national systems that our leaders seem to envy.

Choice of doctors would be determined by whether doctors belong to the available managed-care groups. Managed care in "gatekeeper" HMO-style systems is crucial to their plan of controlling health care costs. Rationing of health care, however, would be the responsibility of the care provider and not directly that of the politicians who passed the law.

The Clinton plan doesn't just threaten the ability to choose one's own doctors. It also reduces peoples' control over their health care by requiring a single benefits package for everyone. The plan would prevent consumers from choosing between buying third-party medical insurance (and choice of level and scope of coverage purchased from private insurers) *and* alternatively choosing to self-insure. Those unhappy with the single plan and wanting different coverage or less coverage would find that option difficult if not impossible.

Criminal penalties in the law would severely limit consumer choice. Consider, for example, the the following provision of Clinton's Health Security Act:

> No health plan, insurer, or any other person may offer to any eligible individual a supplemental health benefit policy that duplicates any coverage provided in the comprehensive package. An entity that knowingly and willfully violates any provision of this section with respect to the offering of a supplemental health benefit policy to any individual shall be subject to a civil monetary penalty (not to exceed $10,000) for such violation.[20]

To have meaningful alternatives, you would have to travel to off-shore medical clinics in, for example, the Caribbean or Mexico. Fortunately, these would be outside the reach of the newly expanded government health care bureaucracy.

Government Control And The Loss Of Real Health Insurance

Largely because of government intervention in health care markets, so-called health insurance has largely become a program for the prepayment of medical expenses. With ClintonCare this would be more pronounced. As with the current operation of the Social Security system, the new payroll tax receipts (employer and employee "premiums") would be immediately used by the health alliances to pay current medical bills.

Real health insurance would be a thing of the past. Under the Clinton plan, the consumers' ability to influence the price they pay for health insurance through life-style choices would come to an end.

Community rating would be mandated. Payroll taxes paid by employers and employees in a particular health alliance would be the same for everyone, given their family status (single, couple, one-parent family, or family with children). Life style, past health record, age or any other measurable risk factor would not be considered. Someone who drinks and takes illegal drugs, who smokes, who is promiscuous, who likes to parachute jump, or who lives a sedentary life and is overweight would pay the same premium as those who watch their diet, exercises regularly and generally practice health-enhancing behaviors.[21]

Under the Clinton plan, the consumers' ability to influence the price they pay for health insurance through life-style choices would come to an end.

Most automobile insurance, life insurance, and casualty insurance are priced in an actuarially sound manner to reflect the risk borne by the insurer. For example, driving records, age, sex, the kind of car we drive, how much and where we drive, and other factors determine the price of automobile insurance. Each driver pays an insurance premium that attempts to capture the expected cost that person brings to a large pool of drivers. In turn, premium payments influence our behavior toward safer driving. (Unfortunately, as a result of state's legislating "no-fault insurance" schemes, automobile insurance has also been sliding in the direction of premiums simply serving as advanced payment for accident claims rather than real insurance.)

A competitive market for risk-adjusted health insurance, where risk can be accurately priced, contributes mightily to the benefits we derive from a free-market economy based on individual freedom, individual responsibility, and private property. The real problem of the very small number of truly uninsurable people should be dealt with directly, for example, by a risk-assignment pool.

Even the President has recently admitted that a significant fraction of the current health problems in the United States is the result of personal behavior, such as the use of drugs and alcohol, not using seat belts, smoking, and other life style choices. Self-destructive behavior patterns are beyond the control of medical science. It is highly unlikely that the Administration's proposal and the expanded health care spending it would require, would buy much in the way of better health. And Clinton adviser Paul Starr recognizes that health care spending in the U.S. would rise from the current 14 percent of GDP to 17 percent in the late 1990s even under the Clinton plan.[22]

Much is made of preventive care in the Clinton plan. But many preventive medical services are already offered free to the poor. Although prenatal care clinics are located throughout Washington, D.C., the city continues to have the highest rate of low-birth-weight deliveries and infant mortality in the nation. Massachusetts offers free immunizations to all its citizens, yet by age two only 62 percent of the state's children are immunized. This is just barely above the national average of 60 percent.[23]

A competitive market for risk-adjusted health insurance, where risk can be accurately priced, contributes mightily to the benefits we derive from a free-market economy based on individual freedom, individual responsibility, and private property.

Community rating would inevitably generate counter-productive incentives, turning for many a temptation to practice health-threatening activities into dangerous habits. With ever rising health care costs, government would eventually try to impose arbitrary controls over behavior and thereby reduce our freedoms even more. Furthermore, when the Clinton plan shifts Medicaid costs for the inner-city poor to the local health alliance, higher "premiums" will be required of employers and employees. A new hidden tax will be paid by urban residents. Businesses, initially stuck with 80 percent of the "premium," will have one more reason to abandon our cities. Have the Clinton's factored in these job losses faced by those who supposedly would be major beneficiaries of the Clinton plan?[24]

It is a monstrous perversion of the notion of fairness to suggest that a clean-living person who makes good choices should pay the same health care premium as the one who does not.

The administration's health care advisers repeatedly claim that community rating is "fair." But it is a monstrous perversion of the notion of fairness to suggest that a clean-living person who makes good choices should pay the same health care premium as the one who does not. A mandated benefit package with a single price for everyone, biased in favor of bureaucratic solutions and against the market, produced this biting commentary by economist Thomas Sowell:

> The truly ugly notion underlying all this is that ordinary people who work and save, in order to be independent, should not be allowed to be better off than those who didn't and who are dependent on the largess of the government.... This is the real meaning of all the lofty talk about how this or that is a 'basic right,' whether or not one has mere money.[25]

Community rating, divorced as it is from personal behavior and life-style choices, and the loss of real, risk-based health insurance would simply accelerate the erosion in social and moral standards we see today.

The Third Party Payment Problem Dooms The Plan

The explosive increase in health care costs is the inevitable result of isolating individual patients from the cost of their care. Third-party payments by private insurance companies and by Medicare and Medicaid contribute to the erroneous view that health care is free.

Although the Clintons talk about a market-oriented reform package that uses private markets, their policy assertions about markets demonstrate little understanding of a real competitive market process. A true market requires cost-conscious consumers evaluating offers to sell by competing suppliers.

Compared to 40 years ago, most of the money spent on personal health care does not come from our own pockets. Third parties now pay 95 percent of hospital bills and about 80 percent of physician bills. On average, less than 20 percent of total health care spending is out-of-pocket by patient-consumers. At the margin, where the decision is made to buy one more procedure or one more office visit, the consumer usually

---

The explosive increase in health care costs is the inevitable result of isolating individual patients from the cost of their care.

---

spends none of his own money. It is "free." Hence, the impact on behavior normally generated by changing market prices is largely absent. Rigid and distorted health care markets are prevented from serving their essential function—to coordinate the self-interested plans of buyers and sellers that, in turn, generate competition, promote efficiency and control costs.

When the price is either zero or just a small fraction of the actual cost of the service, the unavoidable result is that the demand for health care is dramatically higher.

The costs of individual decisions are borne by others in the form of higher insurance premiums and higher taxes for everyone. On the other hand, if someone fails to go to a doctor or declines an optional medical procedure, for whatever reason, the benefits from the resources "saved" accrue to others. Market prices, thus, are not permitted to serve as signals measuring the real costs of our spending choices. A basic function of the marketplace, to hold people responsible for their behavior, is lost. The end result finds everyone living at the expense of everyone else.

The Myth That Health Care Is Free

The notion persists among consumers that health care is far cheaper than it really is. The direct and indirect out-of-pocket costs of care for an average American family, including the Medicare tax, policy deductibles and co-payments, and other out-of-pocket expenses are about $2,000 per year. But the total societal cost in 1992, including other taxes, tax subsidies, and the contributions of employers, was actually almost twice as high. The simple fact is that, as individuals and families, we grossly underestimate the costs of our health care. That leads, without question, to our spending more on medical care than we otherwise would.[26]

Public opinion polls in Great Britain indicate that about 88 percent of the British public prefers the National Health Service (NHS) to the U.S. system. This very favorable view of the NHS exists despite objective evidence that British health care is inferior to the U.S., especially for serious illnesses. Tellingly, many Brits take the option of supplementing the NHS system with private insurance. Long waits for surgery and the limited availability of modern medical technology, for example CAT-scan and MRI technology, impair the quality of care people receive in the NHS.

The costs of individual decisions are borne by others in the form of higher insurance premiums and higher taxes for everyone.

British perception, however, is that their system does not cost very much. In public opinion polls, 60 percent of the British public said they thought that the entire cost of the NHS was met from a payroll tax they call the "insurance stamp." When these polls were taken in the 1970s, how much of the total cost of the NHS was, in fact, covered by the insurance stamp? Only 8.5 percent! Furthermore, most people believed that two-thirds of the insurance stamp was paid by the employer, failing to recognize the view of economists that in the long run employer mandates are really paid by the workers. Underestimating the cost of socialized medicine by a factor of twelve, it is no wonder the British favor their system to ours.[27]

The end result finds everyone living at the expense of everyone else.

Many people believe that health care is a special case, that health care must be free as a "human right" in the name of fairness. But is food less important? Most of us, thankfully, would believe it absurd to offer food free after a $100 deductible had been met. We would all buy lots of filet mignon steak, lobster and exotic French cheeses. Total food expenditures would skyrocket. Food prices would rise, a cost-control problem would materialize, and, happily for politicians, there would be a "food crisis." Filet mignon would be in short supply and in general the quality of food available would decline.

The Clinton solution? They would impose a single food plan for everyone with a common menu for each meal. Then a National Food Board would be created that would impose a global ceiling on food expenditures. Next they would mandate a payroll tax on employers who would turn the money over to food-purchasing alliances that would then pay the grocery stores. Long lines at the supermarkets, however, would prove conclusively that free enterprise was failing to meet the food needs of our population. Hence a bold new government program, "The Plentiful Food Supply Act," would be enacted.

Most of us, thankfully, would believe it absurd to offer food free after a $100 deductible had been met.

But the fraction of the Gross Domestic Product spent on food would be rising. A government-mandated global budget would then require price controls on specific items, but that would only intensify the food shortages that had begun to appear. A formal system of rationing would be imposed. And now either grocery stores or the National Food Board would have to allocate "fair" food shares to all Americans.

Government's massive intervention in the health-care market is the real problem that needs to be addressed. Medicare and Medicaid, tax incentives that encourage buying more health care than we would without the tax advantage, and a proliferation of regulations and paperwork that reduce competition and significantly raise health-care prices, are the root causes that need changing. Every time government uses its power to interfere with markets, it sets in motion a train of events that cause even more serious problems which then lead to even more government solutions. The pattern has been repeated *ad nauseam*.

Which brings us to another important question. Why is a multi-tier health care system unfair, where some people spend more and some less, some search for the very highest quality care while others want "Volkswagen medicine"? Isn't that how markets work? Fortunately, in a free society in which effort, self-improvement, perseverance, and, yes, luck, determine the value that the market places on our economic contribution, most of us do *not* consider choices based on income or different tastes unfair. While some dine at the finest French restaurants, others eat a Big Mac at McDonalds; while some people own a BMW, many of us choose a Honda Civic or a Chevrolet Cavalier. Indeed, because value is subjective and very personal, in a free society some even choose to drive a BMW while eating at McDonalds. Others elect to own an expensive home while driving an old Toyota Tercel. Isn't that what freedom is all about? Freedom simply asks that individuals assume personal responsibility for their actions.

Global Budgets And Price Controls
Necessarily Mean Rationing Health Care

Economist Alain Enthoven, an early proponent of "managed competition," has stated that the Health Security Act's global budget, a government decision on how much the nation could spend on health care each year, is "akin to bombing from 35,000 feet." It has the advantage that "from your very high office in Washington, D.C. you do not see the people you are killing."[28] In other words, effective price controls have always required non-price rationing. The "new" Democrats at the Democratic Leadership Council recognize this immutable fact: a global budget with price controls, if nothing is done to "change the system's inflationary incentives,...would be like putting a lid on a boiling pot without first turning down the heat."[29]

Price controls do not rescind the law of scarcity. Devoting more resources to purpose 'A' leaves fewer for use 'B.' When Clinton and his stable of planners say it won't happen, they are defying the unanimous verdict of history. Holding prices down both encourages consumers to demand more and discourages suppliers from supplying as much. Our experiences with energy price controls during the 1970s and the resulting fuel oil, natural gas, and gasoline shortages are prime examples of the perverse incentives that the government price controls gave to consumers and producers.

Nevertheless, the Clinton brain trust repeatedly denies that their scheme contains price controls or even needs them. In their August 1993 document "Health Care Update: The Need for Health Care Reform," the administration's answers to hypothetical questions were as follows:

Q. How are you going to control costs?

A. [The plan]... will limit the growth of health care premiums. It will insist that the insurance companies and drug companies charge fair prices.

Q. Won't a government budget on health care mean rationing?

A. No. That's just another scare tactic from the people who profit from the status quo. Its a smokescreen...

The Clinton plan will control costs in a number of ways... [by] putting a limit on how much the insurance companies can raise your premiums... [But not to worry] The [global] budget is merely a backstop to ensure that costs don't continue to spiral out of control.[30]

Or, at another point in this same document: "Costs will be kept low by market forces [i.e. managed competition enforced by the large purchasing alliances] and *guaranteed by a fail safe budget enforcement mechanism* to limit the rate of premium increases."[31]   If health care spending exceeds projections and premium monies prove inadequate, the Health Security Act requires state governments and insurers to make "automatic, mandatory, non-discretionary reductions in payments" to providers.[32] If it looks and acts like a global budget constraint then it is a global budget constraint.

Government's massive intervention in the health-care market is the real problem that needs to be addressed.

Controlling premiums paid to acceptable health care providers would require that managed-care providers, in turn, establish ceilings paid for particular procedures. According to the Health Care Security Act submitted to Congress, medical spending that exceeded per-capita limits set by the National Health Board would require that HMOs and other providers cut payments to doctors, staff and hospitals to stay within budget. The purchasing alliances that report to the individual states and the National Health Board would have the legal power to establish a schedule of doctors fees, and doctors could not legally accept more. The bill also gives the Secretary of Health and Human Services, super-liberal Donna Shalala, authority to set a controlled price for every new drug. For the Clinton plan to succeed with the outrageous and unrealizable claim that only a moderate sin tax would be necessary, aggregate budget limits and price controls are absolutely essential.

What are we to make of the Clinton administration's tendency to blame greedy capitalists for escalating health care costs? Hillary Clinton has been especially vocal on this score. Before a national television audience and in an accusatory tone Mrs. Clinton blamed rising health care costs on "unconscionable profiteering" and "price gouging." Nor did the President mince words in his campaign document, "Putting People First: A National Economic Strategy for America." The rapid increase in health care costs, alleges our President, is the result of greed by the pharmaceutical and insurance industries: "What we need are leaders who are willing to take on the insurance companies, the drug companies, and the health-care bureaucracies and bring health-care costs down."[33]

This outrageous charge conveniently ignores the indisputable fact that government-controlled Medicare and Medicaid programs along with third-party payments have been the driving forces behind rising health care costs. And the President's bureaucratic solution would at least triple the size of the existing federal health bureaucracy.

According to the Health Care Security Act submitted to Congress, medical spending that exceeded per-capita limits set by the National Health Board would require that HMOs and other providers cut payments to doctors, staff and hospitals to stay within budget.

Apparently in a more reflective moment, the President spoke honestly to doctors at Johns Hopkins University: "We'll never get the cost of health care down to where it is in other countries as long as we have higher rates of teen pregnancies and higher rates of low-birth weight babies and higher rates of AIDS, and most important of all, higher rates of violence."[34]

The President's sober judgment suggests a few important questions. If the great majority of Americans are satisfied with their existing health insurance, and if social and moral issues will influence the extent to which rising health care costs can be brought under control, then why do we need radical *political* surgery on the whole system? Why don't we try market-oriented changes in the structure of incentives which we know would work? Why must all Americans buy this politically contrived bureaucratic monster?

The Financing Plan Is Fantasy

Senator Patrick Moynihan (D, New York) has appropriately called the financing of the Clinton plan pure "fantasy." The scheme to finance the new, universal "entitlement" assumes that increases in the global health care budget can be held to the rate of inflation in the late 1990s and into the next century. Even with the Clinton plan in place, the administration admits that total spending would continue to rise as a fraction of GDP late into the 1990s.

For the Clinton plan to succeed with the outrageous and unrealizable claim that only a moderate sin tax would be necessary, aggregate budget limits and price controls are absolutely essential.

Certain unavoidable facts about American society make their scenario highly unlikely. First, as already noted, spending on health care tends to rise faster than income as standards of living rise. Second, the American population will continue to age, and as we live longer the demand will grow for drugs to ease our geriatric ailments, for sophisticated diagnostic equipment, for technology-driven surgical techniques, and for high-tech cures for cancer and other diseases.

Third, the demand for long-term care by the aging will also continue to be an important force. In 1992, nursing home expenditures increased by 12.5 percent. In 1990 there were 3.3 million Americans over the age of 84. This number will exceed 7 million by 2010.

And finally, medical progress is expensive. It would be slowed by the Clinton plan, but the search for cures to diseases that claim human lives would not stop. "An aging society demanding more and better health care from an industry searching for more and better cures," according to health care analyst J. D. Kleinke, "quite simply flies in the face of the [Clinton administration's] health care inflation fantasy."[35]

Under The Clinton Plan
The Quality Of Health Care Will Suffer

It is well documented that there is always a decrease in the quality of health care following the appearance of health care rationing in nationally-directed, bureaucratic regimes.[36] Rationing and lower-quality medicine would also occur with the Clinton plan. Here's why.

First, expanded coverage at low out-of-pocket prices would greatly increase the demand for health care. Second, the limits on premium revenues going to health care providers would require them to cut corners to meet the bureaucracy's arbitrary spending ceilings. The choice and availability of drugs and laboratory tests might be reduced. Office visits would be shortened. Non-emergency surgery would be postponed or denied. For example, a 1988 Department of Health and Human Services report estimated 540,000 Medicare patients received poor-quality hospital care due to Medicare's price controls. Possibilities for restricting access would be limitless. And, remember, anyone who tried to shift to another plan would be breaking the law.

Third, everyone would be pushed into managed-care type organizations such as HMOs and PPOs. It would be easier to ration care through "gatekeepers," who must first control costs by staying within their budgets set by a health alliance. Serving patients would come after the goal of meeting budgets. Doctors, hospitals and other care providers would be cast in the villains' role of deciding whether or not to provide care. The politicians, including the President, would be roughly four levels of bureaucracy removed from the physician who actually does the rationing.

Stories of physicians being dropped from HMO and PPO plans because they practice "high-cost medicine" are now widespread. Not surprisingly, law suits are being brought by these physicians on the grounds that their termination interferes with the practice of quality medicine and the doctor-patient relationship. Politicians, however, would deny any responsibility for the shortage of monies and the waiting lists for "optional" surgery.

If the great majority of Americans are happy with their existing health insurance, and if social and moral issues will influence the extent to which rising health care costs can be brought under control, then why do we need radical political surgery on the whole system?

Finally, drug research and innovative new technologies would be discouraged, adding further to the problem of deteriorating quality. Just as in Canada and Britain, Americans without serious illnesses would be generally pleased with the ready availability (admittedly with a long office wait) of a general practitioner. But heaven help the four percent of the population each year who have real, life-threatening medical problems. It does, however, make good political sense. Politicians need majorities, not the small minority who are seriously ill.

Today the British, Canadians, Saudis, and people from all over the world come to the United States with their serious health problems. Seattle, Minneapolis, Detroit, and Buffalo, for example, have thousands of Canadian patients. Quebec premier Robert Bourassa, for example, came to the U.S. for treatment of his skin cancer. Jordan's king arrived in the U.S. early in 1994 for medical treatment. The quality of America's health care system, where advanced technologies and modern well-staffed facilities improve the chances of cure and survival, is recognized worldwide. Where will *we* go after the Clinton plan has destroyed the finest medical care system in the world?

Socialized Medicine Is Not Good Enough For Congress

To rub even more salt in the wound, although many in Congress believe they should impose a government-controlled, health-care system on the rest of us, they don't believe they should have to live under it. Senate Majority Leader George Mitchell (D., Maine) has introduced a bill (S. 1227) that includes a specific requirement that Congress and all federal employees be exempt from any national health care plan.[37]

The politicians, including the President, would be roughly four levels of bureaucracy removed from the physician who actually does the rationing.

Our elected officials are famous for the practice of exempting themselves from what they mandate for the rest of us. Congress has exempted itself from, among others laws, the Civil Rights Act, the Americans with Disabilities Act, the Family and Medical Leave Act, the Social Security system (FICA), the Age Discrimination and Employment Act, the National Labor Relations Act, and the Ethics in Government Act. James Madison, a leading framer of the U.S. Constitution, sought to protect us from our political leaders. In *The Federalist*,

> *Our elected officials are famous for the practice of exempting themselves from what they mandate for the rest of us.*

he stated that Congress should "make no law which will not have its full operation on themselves and their friends, as well as on the great mass of society."[38] He wanted to avoid the situation that George Orwell described in his book *Animal Farm*, where some animals were more equal than others.

A dual system would be similar to that which prevailed in the former Soviet Union and other Eastern European communist countries. Communist party officials and key bureaucrats received medical care at one place and the proletariat at another. Hospitals for the elite were well stocked with the latest technology and modern conveniences, even frequently with drugs and equipment purchased in the West. The masses in these Communist utopias suffered abominable shortages of drugs and medical equipment and more health care rationing than in the elite's system.[39]

The Employer Mandate Means Lower Wages And Fewer Jobs

Under ClintonCare, employers would be forced to pay 80 percent of their employees' health insurance costs, the employee 20 percent. The latest version caps a company's contribution between 3.5 and 7.9 percent of payroll, depending on the size of the firm and the average wage paid. Workers are falsely led to believe they are getting something for twenty cents on the dollar. The Clintons and their advisers also seem to believe that employers would really bear the burden of this new tax. The President, however, would do well to heed his own warning to the American people that health care is not "paid for by the tooth fairy."

The employer mandate is in fact a large tax on American labor. As I have stated earlier, the burden of the tax ultimately rests with employees, not the employer. With the passage of time, higher labor costs for business make take-home pay grow more slowly or even fall; to the extent it doesn't fall, many workers will lose their jobs. A worker's pay is measured by the individual's productivity, and whatever a company is mandated to pay for health care benefits must necessarily come out of money wages or other employee benefits.

The employer mandate is in fact a large tax on American labor.

The requirement that companies pay up to 7.9 percent of payroll in new taxes would be especially hard on lower-wage industries. While the tax would be capped in the beginning at 3.5 percent of payroll for firms that pay the minimum wage, the fact remains that it would be a hefty tax increase for those companies not currently providing health care insurance. Thousands of small firms and a number of large businesses are in this situation. The new payroll tax would be a larger fraction of the low-wage worker's total compensation and therefore have a larger impact on a low-wage company's labor costs. One study estimated that labor costs in the restaurant industry would rise by more than

19 percent, in household services by 33 percent.[40]

During a transition period following the imposition of the employer mandate, companies' labor costs would be higher and their profits lower. Asked in a Congressional hearing last August about the survival problems mandates raise for small businesses, Hillary Clinton (a.k.a. Marie Antoinette) sniffed: "I can't go out and save every undercapitalized entrepreneur in America." That "undercapitalized employer" might be your employer that she dismisses so easily. America's businesses are not asking her to save them; they are asking that she get government off their back.

What an irony? A new health care entitlement mandated by government could cause the loss of millions of jobs, mostly for those whom this administration claims to care about.

Economists June O'Neill and David O'Neill estimate that higher labor costs under the Clinton plan would result in the loss of up to 3.1 million jobs. Even the administration admits to the possible loss of more than 500,000 jobs. The job losses will be concentrated in low-wage industries such as eating and drinking establishments, personal services, agricultural and other retailing industries. What an irony? A new health care entitlement mandated by government could cause the loss of millions of jobs, mostly for those whom this administration claims to care about.

Actually, many experts believe the Clinton reform plan, if adopted, would quickly require an employer payroll tax of at least 10 or 12 percent, not 7.9 percent. If so, labor costs would be pushed even higher, wages would fall even more, and even more jobs would be destroyed. The tax currently averages 13.4 percent in Germany.

Economist Martin Feldstein has also shown that the shrinkage in taxable wages and salaries that would accompany reduced hiring and rising layoffs would have undesirable budgetary effects. He has estimated that under the Clinton plan 1997 wages would be reduced by $115 billion and that this would cut federal tax revenues by as much as $49 billion—$24 billion less in personal income tax collections, $16 billion less in employer-employee Social Security tax receipts and $9 billion less in payroll health premium receipts. The federal budget deficit would increase, and the new health care plan would become even more difficult to finance.

In summary, the Clinton health care reform plan not only puts the government in control of our health but also imposes additional burdens that would reduce job growth and, at least temporarily, reduce business cash flow, hinder capital investment and therefore hurt productivity. And it would cause, according to their own criteria, a very unfair distribution of the burdens, in particular on the low-income, working poor. Millions of uninsured would be replaced by the prospect of millions of unemployed. These adverse and ignored consequences capture the misguided genius of the administration's national economic planners, in particular health care chief-of-staff Ira Magaziner and Secretary of Labor Robert Reich.

The Administration Hopes To Keep This Massive New Tax Out Of The Federal Budget

Demonstrating an utter lack of integrity by the Clinton White House, they seek to keep the outlays and receipts of their plan out of the federal budget. Early in December 1993, according to the *Washington Post,* the Congressional Budget Office agreed to the administration's urging that mandatory employer "premiums" as a fraction of payroll not be counted as taxes and therefore be exempt from budgetary oversight.[41]   If they were to succeed, hundreds of billions of dollars would not be subject to conventional budgetary review and would be shuffled through purchasing alliances to managed-care health care providers at the arbitrary whim of the new National Health Board.

In 1993, adding about $650 billion in U.S. health care spending to the unified federal budget, as well as the payroll taxes being used to finance it, would amount to a startling forty percent increase in the size of the federal budget.

In 1993, adding about $650 billion in U.S. health care spending to the unified federal budget (equals total U.S. health care spending minus Medicare and Medicaid spending on health care), as well as the payroll taxes being used to finance it, would amount to a startling *forty* percent increase in the size of the federal budget! "Proposing that a major new tax not be called a tax is a first step," Martin Feldstein warns, "toward a new form of fiscal irresponsibility in which future tax increases would occur automatically without legislative action."[42] Leaving the Clinton monster off budget would allow health-care spending and financing to be in a never-never land without either the discipline of market pressures or Congressional budget oversight.

With the prospects of rising federal budget deficits at the end of the century and record high tax burdens on the American people, it is understandable why this administration must do their best to keep the new payroll tax out of the federal budget. But the deception must be recognized for what it is. Such a power grab represents the latest and by far the largest attempt ever by government to use mandates to end-run the limits taxpayers have tried to place on government's ability to tax and spend. Politicians hand out more "entitlements" to increase their chance of reelection, while trying to avoid the unpleasant task of raising the money to pay for them. There is no end to the good that do-gooders will do with other people's money. And even more so when it is called a premium rather than a tax.

Claiming that costs will be controlled, while creating the illusion that health care is "free," or almost free, is an impossible promise.

Clinton's Health Security Act, if passed, would be a disaster for America. The whole monstrosity collapses as soon as the American people discover that there is no tooth fairy and that it is people, not companies, who pay taxes. The fraudulent scam of an employer mandate to raise hundreds of billions of dollars follows in lock-step fashion with a plan that promises a massive new "entitlement" for all Americans. The liberal benefits package in the Clinton plan (dental care, vision care, mental health therapy, physical therapy, drug and alcohol dependency programs, a new Medicare drug benefit, long-term care, preventative care programs as well as conventional hospital and physician services) will only drive demand even higher.

Claiming that costs will be controlled, while creating the illusion that health care is "free," or almost free, is an impossible promise. ClintonCare is bamboozlement like no other, and if enacted, would cause untold harm.

CHAPTER FOUR

Market-Oriented
Health Care Reform

The Clinton Administration's health care reform plan is based on a wrong assumption—that self-interested behavior can be ignored, regulated, or possibly eliminated. But from all available evidence, self- interest is part of human nature. To induce people to behave in ways that benefit others, people must face appropriate rewards and penalties. When seeking health care, people show the same self-interested behavior as they do in other markets. The problem is that they are currently receiving counterproductive signals. Instead of increasing regulation and bureaucracy, government policy should empower individuals to be conscientious shoppers for medical care. Incentives should be used to channel self-interested behavior in desirable directions. Individuals should be held accountable for their purchasing decisions in a real free-market environment by bearing the costs of their choices, not by dumping these costs on others.

Using The Market To Control Escalating Health Care Costs

A market-oriented approach to health care reform would redirect health-care spending by giving consumers both the freedom to choose how to spend their own money and the incentive to take responsibility for their choices. Market solutions require a reduced role for government in the health care system. Policies should be encouraged that create an environment in which real market institutions can thrive.

When seeking health care, people show the same self-interested behavior as they do in other markets. The problem is that they are currently receiving counterproductive signals.

ClintonCare, in contrast, would greatly expand government regulation and create new government bureaucracies to hopefully control health care costs. Simultaneously, a centralized, government-oriented plan would further erode personal responsibility.

The National Center for Policy Analysis (NCPA) has identified five major goals that would be necessary for a health care system founded on individual freedom and the discipline associated with competitive market solutions.[43]

(1) Transfer power from large institutions and impersonal bureaucracies to individuals.

(2) Restore the buyer/seller relationship to patients and medical suppliers, so that patients (rather than third party insurers) become the principal buyers of health care.

(3) Create institutions in which patients (as much as possible) spend their own money, rather

than someone else's, when they purchase health care.

(4) Remove health care (as much as possible) from the political arena, in which well-organized special interests can cause great harm to the rest of us.

(5) Subject the health care sector to the rigors of competition and create market-based institutions in which individuals reap the full benefits of their good decisions and bear the full costs of their bad ones.

The Issue Of Informed Consumers In The Medical Marketplace

Myth notwithstanding, universal access to health care is not the issue. Americans, even the poorest, do not go without medical care. Gun-shot wounds and drug overdoses are treated in urban hospitals with the most advanced technology. Federal law requires most emergency rooms to accept patients regardless of their ability to pay. As economist Thomas Sowell has observed: "We already have universal access to medical care. You can't get more universal than universal."[44]

We are supposedly not smart enough to pick a doctor or shop for the lowest price for a medical procedure. Yet, we are continually reminded of how important it is that we vote in elections for candidates who will vote for hundreds of separate bills of which we can have only limited, if any, knowledge.

But the paternalistic view that consumers are incompetent is an important factor in the health-care debate. Many people reject market approaches to controlling rising health care costs in the misguided view that shopping for medical care is too complex for individuals to make wise choices. We are deemed helpless without the assistance of big government. We are supposedly not smart enough to pick a doctor or shop for the lowest price for a medical procedure. Yet, we are continually reminded of how important it is that we vote in elections for candidates who will vote for hundreds of separate bills of which we can have only limited, if any, knowledge. As John Goodman and Gerald Musgrave have noted in *Patient Power,* "If choosing a physician is complex, choosing a politician who will appoint a bureaucrat to choose a physician [for us] is even more complex."[45]

Empowering health care consumers follows from the proposition that no one cares more about us than we do.

The case for the free market rests on the proposition that suppliers are motivated by profit to serve consumers. Consumers, spending their own money, are motivated to be informed shoppers. As in markets for furniture, automobiles, automobile mechanics, stereo components, and restaurants, the solution that invariably works is to have consumers choosing between alternative uses of their money. In competitive markets, both buyers and sellers are forced to acknowledge the costs of their actions and are therefore motivated to become better informed.

Empowering health care consumers follows from the proposition that no one cares more about us than we do. Recently, Senator Phil Gramm, R-Texas, was debating one of the defenders of the Clinton program. Gramm said that no one cared about his grandchildren's health as much as he did. The Clinton spokesman said that was not true, that he too cared about their health care. Asked Gramm, "What are their names?"

More than 90 percent of all medical care decisions are made in non-crisis situations. Our task should be to create a market environment in which doctors, outpatient clinics, hospitals and other suppliers are interested in providing consumers with accurate information about health care alternatives. Notice the considerable effort companies devote to getting our business in other competitive environments. And we forget—one of the unsung marvels of a market economy—that suppliers, when responding to the special concerns of a minority of informed consumers, generate product quality and price benefits that accrue to all buyers, informed or not.

The business of providing useful, market information is itself big business. Many companies have "cost management programs" that provide information to their employees on life-style issues and alternatives available in the medical market place. The company behind *Consumer Reports*, for example, has published *The Savvy Patient: How to Be an Active Participant in Your Medical Care* to assist patient-consumers in making choices.[46] The new era of interactive multimedia promises untold possibilities. Compact Disk (CD) technology and the modem in our personal computers are already making available medical diagnostic services to consumers.

Current Tax Laws Discourage Free Market Solutions

More than 92 percent of Americans who have private health insurance receive it through their employer. Employer-provided health care benefits receive a large subsidy because they are a deductible expense to the employer and are not treated as taxable income to the worker. Employees receive health care (and other) benefits on which they do not pay federal taxes or state income taxes. The result? Ninety-seven percent of individuals to whom tax-subsidized medical insurance is available from their employer have health insurance. But only 33 percent of those who must buy health insurance out of their after-tax income are insured.[47]

For someone in the 28 percent federal income tax bracket, who is also paying social security and Medicare (FICA) taxes of 15.3 percent, and a 6 percent state income tax, the value of a pretax, health care benefit is almost twice the value of an equivalent increase in wage and salary income. If it were possible for workers to substitute higher wages for the expensive health care policy, employees would demand an increase in pretax wages of almost $2 to make it worthwhile to give up $1 worth of health care benefits.   Even low-wage employees, who pay no federal income tax or state income tax and just pay FICA taxes, currently find the employer-based subsidized health care benefit almost twenty percent more valuable than the value of the same dollar increase in wages.[48]

Subsidized health-care benefits to the employee, therefore, lead to excessive spending on health care insurance.   In 1992 the aggregate value of this tax subsidy to the employees of companies offering employer-provided medical plans amounted to about $65 billion in lost revenue to the U.S. Treasury . Tax rates, therefore, needed to be correspondingly higher to recover the lost revenues, and everybody, whether receiving subsidized health care benefits or not, paid these higher taxes.

The adverse consequences of the subsidy are predictable. Individuals are motivated to "buy" costly policies. Companies, in turn, are motivated to provide, fancy, bells-and-whistles health care policies where the real value of the benefits package, minus tax subsidy, is only half its social cost. Simply put, our tax laws encourage wasteful "first dollar coverage," low deductibles and low co-payments.

Federal tax law generally prevents trading health insurance and other employee benefits for higher wages. More often than not, employee benefit laws strongly encourage or even require companies to offer the same bells-and-whistles policy to all employees. In this artificial world, where individuals are not free to choose how to divide their compensation package between wages and benefits, the incentive to be a cost-conscious consumer of health care is absent. Indeed, an employee who acted as a prudent buyer of health care, and, for example, opted for a policy with a higher deductible and fewer benefits, would have to pay additional taxes on the resulting increase in money wages. The worker would lose the tax subsidy currently available to employee benefits.

Simply put, our tax laws encourage wasteful "first dollar coverage," low deductibles and low co-payments.

The existing employer-based health care insurance system is patently unfair.[49] First, the tax subsidy is only available to employees who work for companies that offer health insurance benefits. The self employed, the unemployed, and those working for companies that do not provide health benefits receive no tax subsidy. (Note: The self-employed are again, in 1994, able to deduct 25 percent of their insurance premium.)

Second, the subsidy is regressive because it is larger the higher the employee's income. One 1992 study estimated, on average, that the value of the tax subsidy to families with very high incomes (the top fifth of the income distribution) equaled $1,560, while low-income families (the bottom fifth of the income distribution), working for a company offering benefits, received a subsidy worth only $270.[50] And, as just noted, someone who is unemployed or working for a company that doesn't provide benefits receives zero subsidy. The existing system penalizes people who purchase their own insurance. Working as an independent contractor,

I am particularly aware of this discrimination against the self-employed.

The current employer-based system not only subsidizes the rich and penalizes the poor and the unemployed, but is a major contributing factor to the growing number of Americans without health insurance.

First, if you lose your job or switch jobs, generally you lose your health insurance.[51] Second, and in combination, 1) the tax code subsidy, 2) the "free" provision of care at the point of consumption by third-party insurers, and 3) the explosive increase in government Medicare and Medicaid outlays that shift costs to private insurers, cause wasteful and excessive spending on health care. Health care costs rise and therefore health insurance premiums rise. Small businesses and their employees and price-sensitive consumers (especially young and healthy individuals) are, as a result, priced out of the market. The number without insurance predictably goes up.

A Market Solution Requires That Health Insurance Be Personal and Portable

For both reasons of fairness and efficiency, Congress needs to change the federal tax code. First, employer-provided health care benefits must be recognized as part of a worker's income, a component in total employee compensation. Employee benefit laws need to be changed so that employees would have the freedom to choose different combinations of taxable wages and *taxable* fringe benefits.

The tax subsidy that provides larger subsidies to the rich than the poor and only to people who work for employers that provide health benefits at the expense of those not so lucky, like the self-employed and unemployed, must be repealed.

Instead, if society believes it desirable to subsidize health care, individuals and families should be given a direct subsidy in the form of a tax credit against their income tax liability. The tax credit would be available to everyone, not just those working for certain businesses.

Employers would be encouraged to offer health care benefit options that provide individuals with a broad range of choices in health insurance coverage. A federal law overriding state government health benefit mandates (such as hairpieces, marriage counseling, and sperm bank deposits[52]) might be required so that companies could offer inexpensive catastrophic policies and other less expensive choices to their employees. State mandates frequently force workers to either purchase a bells-and-whistles plan or remain uninsured. It has been estimated that one out of every four people without health insurance has been priced out of the market by the cost-increasing effects of state-mandated benefits.[53]

In this artificial world, where individuals are not free to choose how to divide their compensation package between wages and benefits, the incentive to be a cost-conscious consumer of health care is absent.

Health insurance policies would be "owned" by employees and therefore follow them, making health insurance both personal and portable. The tax credit to individuals should be limited. This would both eliminate the larger tax benefit currently available to higher-income families and, importantly, encourage people to buy high-deductible and therefore less-expensive policies. "Individualized" health insurance choices would also encourage people to substitute self-insurance in place of third-party health insurance. The tax penalty in the current system for people self-insuring against health care risks would be eliminated, as described below.

Ultimately, empowering individuals is the key to getting the cost-conscious consumer of medical care back into the decision-making loop. Individuals should become the real customers of physicians.

Medisave Accounts Will Encourage Self Insurance And Therefore Prudent Consumption Of Health Care Services

The tax credit, in addition to financing premiums on catastrophic, third-party health insurance, would also be available for funds deposited in special medisave accounts, which would be used to pay small medical bills. These balances would grow tax-free and be the property of the individual or family. For most people they would grow over time because medical expenses would be less than the growth in their tax-subsidized deposits. Eventually accumulated funds would be used to meet the higher medical expenses associated with age or post-retirement medical costs; otherwise they would become part of the person's estate.

The current employer-based system not only subsidizes the rich and penalizes the poor and the unemployed, but is a major contributing factor to the growing number of Americans without health insurance.

Consumers would be empowered to shop carefully for their health-care needs. They would realize that prudent, cost-conscious decisions, healthy life styles, and preventive medical tests would save *their own* money. As a result, the market for health care would be revitalized. Medical care providers would, in turn, be motivated to respond to patients rather than to big third-party insurance companies. The only cost-control system that has ever worked, the free-market system, would be given free reign. The National Center for Policy Analysis has estimated that widespread use of medisave accounts could reduce total health care spending in the U.S. by almost one-fourth.[54]

Ultimately, empowering individuals is the key to getting the cost-conscious consumer of medical care back into the decision-making loop. Individuals should become the real customers of physicians.

With individuals paying small medical bills out of their medisave accounts, administrative costs now associated with third-party billing would be significantly reduced. Families would pay their bills from their medisave account with a health-care debit card. Administrative costs of private health insurance are about 12 percent of premiums. One estimate suggests that administrative costs in 1990 would have been reduced by up to $33 billion if medisave accounts had been in general use.[55]

There are other important benefits of tax-supported medisave accounts. Third-party health insurance costs would be lower as premiums decrease for policies with higher deductibles. Insurance would therefore become more affordable and reduce the number of people who have, under the existing system, been priced out of the market for catastrophic insurance.

Self-insurance through medisave accounts would be portable. Money in the account would belong to the individual or family. During periods of unemployment, account balances would be available to meet small medical expenses *and* also to continue premium payments on a catastrophic policy. As medisave account balances grew over time, families could raise deductibles on their catastrophic third-party policy and save even more in the way of lower insurance premiums.

Medisave accounts would also be used to meet expenses devoted to preventive medicine, including, for example, tests and examinations for breast and prostate cancer.

A bonus benefit of medisave accounts would be the likely increase in the U.S. domestic saving rate. Rather than the current pay-as-you-go health insurance system, more and more being dominated by Medicare and Medicaid, the American people would increase their personal saving to meet health care expenses during their working lives and during their retirement. A higher rate of U.S. saving would add to our investment in machinery, computers and other capital goods which would raise living standards and strengthen America's international competitiveness.

Consumers would be empowered to shop carefully for their health-care needs. They would realize that prudent, cost-conscious decisions, healthy life styles, and preventive medical tests would save their own money.

The so-called health "insurance" most of us have today is in fact the prepayment for current consumption of medical care. Real insurance, the actuarial hedging of measurable risk, has almost disappeared from the offerings of third-party private insurance companies. President Clinton would have us take the very last step in this direction with community rating. Everyone in a health plan would pay the same "premium" (i.e., tax), regardless of life-style choices, occupation, age, or medical history.

A market-oriented reform package, which changes the tax laws in order to individualize health care insurance and encourage people to self-insure with medisave accounts, would also reinvigorate the market for real health insurance. As with life insurance, casualty insurance and most automobile insurance, competitive insurance markets would encourage desirable health-enhancing and cost-reducing changes in the consumer's behavior. Premiums would be based on life style and other objective factors, and health-threatening behaviors would not be subsidized by the rest of us.

The benefits of medisave accounts are not hypothetical. They have been used in Singapore since 1984. Consumers there have taken responsibility for their own health care purchases, demonstrating that health care markets can be competitive like other markets and that medisave accounts can produce desirable outcomes. Being a forced system in Singapore, deposits have grown rapidly. The use of medisave funds to meet health care expenses have also grown, quadrupling for example between 1985 and 1988.[56]

Premiums would be based on life style and other objective factors, and health-threatening behaviors would not be subsidized by the rest of us.

In spite of disincentives caused by the current federal tax code and by state benefit laws, some American companies have been experimenting with bringing market pressures and consumer self-interest to bear on their high health-care costs. Dominion Resources, Inc. of Richmond, Virginia employs a package with high deductibles, after-tax employee deposits to be used to meet medical expenses (akin to medisave accounts but unfortunately without the tax-credit encouragement described above), and a program in which the practice of preventive medicine is rewarded.[57] Forbes, Inc., publisher of *Forbes* magazine and Golden Rule Insurance Company of Indianapolis, Indiana, among others, have been experimenting with similar programs, and they are working to control health care costs.[58]

How A Medisave Account System Would Work

Here is a simple numerical example of how (1) catastrophic third-party insurance for large health care expenditures combined with (2) medisave accounts for small bills would work.

Depending on revenue impacts on the federal budget *and* society's decision about the extent to which health care should be subsidized, each individual and family would have a federal income tax credit equal to some fraction of a ceiling dollar amount of health care spending. People would be encouraged to use high-deductible policies by limiting the amount of the health care tax credit that could apply to third-party insurance. One approach would be to make the maximum amount of money eligible for the tax credit equal the deductible on a family's catastrophic policy up to some limit, say, $3,000 for a family.

Assume one family buys a policy with a deductible of $200 and a 20 percent co-payment on the next $2,000 of medical expenses. The annual premium, let's say, is $3,000 (under the revised tax code purchased with after-tax income). This family would have a tax credit reducing its tax liability by $200, the amount of the deductible.

Another family buys a policy with a $2,000 deductible and a 20 percent co-payment on the next $2,000 of medical expenses. Let's say the annual premium for this high-deductible policy is $1,200. The high-deductible policy would save the family $1,800 in premium payments relative to the family with the low-deductible policy. This family would have a tax credit of $2,000. The credit would buy the catastrophic, high-deductible policy *and* subsidize a medisave deposit of $800 ($2,000 - $1,200). In this example, if a family bought a policy with a higher, $3,000 deductible, their catastrophic policy premium would be even lower *and* their tax credit would be larger. In turn their annual subsidized medisave deposit could be larger.

Continuing with the example, if each family now had an illness causing medical bills equal to $4,000, how would the above two situations differ? With the low-deductible policy the family's out-of-pocket costs would be $3,000 for the insurance premium, $200 for the deductible and $400 (20% of the next $2,000) as a co-payment for a total of $3,600. A tax credit of $200 would reduce the net outlay to $3,400.

The high-deductible policy would require the family to pay an insurance premium of $1,200, a $2,000 deductible, and a co-payment of $400 (20% of the next $2,000). With premium savings of $1,800, this family's out-of-pocket expenditures would also be $3,600. But this would be significantly offset by the $2,000 federal tax credit for a net outlay of $1,600. In this hypothetical example, the net costs are much lower for the family with the high-deductible policy.

The medisave account balances, which become the private property of the family, would grow tax-free as do existing Individual Retirement Accounts (IRA).

If, during the year, neither family experienced health care expenses, which would be the case for a majority of families, especially younger people, the family with the high deductible would have a tax-free medisave account balance of $800 at the end of the year. With the passage of time, self-insurance through growing medisave account balances would empower individuals to take charge of their health care. Moreover, consumers shopping conscientiously would also generate the other benefits of self-insurance enumerated earlier.

Out-of-pocket medical expenses of most Americans with high-deductible health insurance policies would be low enough that they would have growing balances in their medisave accounts with a maximum tax credit of $3,000 for a family.[59]   As we have already noted, the medisave account balances, which become the private property of the family, would grow tax-free as do existing Individual Retirement Accounts (IRA). Visualize the average young family depositing $1,000 or more each year in their medisave account and watching it grow at compound interest each year.

Using accumulated medisave account balances in combination with other funds saved in a separate or related program specifically devoted to financing post-retirement medical expenses, we would eventually replace Medicare for the elderly with a private, self-financed, market-driven system.

The growth of medisave account balances would be a function of (1) society's collective decision about the amount of subsidized health-care spending; (2) the program's impact on federal outlays and revenues; (3) the extent to which current government outlays on health care such as Medicare, Medicaid, and other federal health spending would be reduced, and (4) the extent to which competitive pressures slow the rise in health care costs. As the market-driven system evolved, government spending on health care would be drastically reduced, if not eliminated.

Subsidized Health Insurance For Those Unable To Pay

If, as a society, we want to subsidize health care through government taxation, then the existing Medicaid program of subsidized health care for the poor should be replaced by direct, cash subsidies to households. The cost to the taxpayer of direct money transfers is explicit and clear to all. Importantly, as previously emphasized, individuals are empowered to shop and be prudent consumers.

Low-income individuals and families who cannot afford a catastrophic, third-party policy and do not have the money to deposit funds in medisave accounts would be subsidized through the use of a negative income tax credit. Examples would include the existing earned-income tax credit for low-income families or alternatively a voucher system.

As the market-driven system evolved, government spending on health care would be drastically reduced, if not eliminated.

The voucher amount or tax credit refund might start, for example, at $3,500 for a family with zero income. Out of this amount, the family would buy a catastrophic policy and deposit the rest in a medisave account. The credit would decrease as a family's income increased and also to the extent that the funds in their medisave account accumulated with the passage of time. Wiser health care choices by the poor would be rewarded. In summary, both Medicare and Medicaid would eventually be privatized.

Needless to say, a market-driven health system would also avoid the massive new bureaucracies that the Clintons want to create, including the new National Health Board which would totally politicize health care in America.

As a result of the empowerment of consumers, both rich and poor, the private sector could then do what it does best: Allocate scarce resources more efficiently *and* harness the self-interest of both consumers and providers to a competitive and therefore efficient health care market place.

Needless to say, a market-driven health system would also avoid the massive new bureaucracies that the Clintons want to create, including the new National Health Board which would totally politicize health care in America. It bears repeating: the administration's planners prefer political solutions and government bureaucracy. Nevertheless, the failure of these kinds of socialistic institutions all around the world surely must suggest to reasonable men and women that finding viable market-oriented adjustments to our health care system would be a more efficient and even fairer approach.

The Problem Of Tort Law Liability And The Waste In Defensive Medicine

A final point needs to be made in this necessarily abbreviated discussion of a market-driven, health care system. The tort system of legal liability is not working well. The threat of being sued for malpractice and having to pay huge settlements to plaintiffs cause doctors' malpractice insurance premiums to increase. In

---

The most efficient solution to the problem of tort liability would be voluntary agreements in the market place.

---

turn, doctors are encouraged to practice "defensive" medicine. The American Medical Association's Center for Health Policy Research found that in 1989 malpractice insurance premiums for physicians reached $4.2 billion and that an additional $12.8 billion was wasted in the practice of defensive medicine, a total of

$17 billion.[60] Jury Verdict Research, Inc. of Solon, Ohio reports that average jury verdicts in 1992 were double what they were in 1987. This explosion in award amounts translates into higher premiums paid by doctors and hospitals and thus results in higher costs for all of us.

But, the tort system remains the patient's greatest protection from malpractice, and this will be especially true if Clinton's plan were to be adopted. Under their plan, rationing of health care and reduced quality would be the predictable outcome. With a socialized system, the patient would probably end up having to sue the National Health Board. Have you ever tried suing the government?

Individuals should be able to give up their opportunity to sue in exchange for compensation.

The favored solution to large malpractice awards that bureaucrats favor is the imposition of arbitrary limits on the rights of plaintiffs in malpractice cases. But bureaucratic decrees are always rigid, invariably inefficient, and frequently unfair. As with the health care reform issue in general, the most efficient solution to the problem of tort liability would be voluntary agreements in the market place.

Consumers of health care should have the same opportunities that they have in other markets. The right to contract is central to the efficient operation of the free market. Individuals should be able to give up their opportunity to sue in exchange for compensation. The compensation might include, for example, lower fees for the service in question and/or a fixed-value insurance policy if the procedure didn't go as expected.

Life and disability insurance companies would write policies for hospitals and physicians who would pay the premiums. The insurance companies would have a strong incentive to monitor the quality of the supplier's performance. Unfortunately, the current system ignores contractual waivers of tort liability. Voluntary exchange is not permitted, and efficiency gains in the marketplace are denied.

CHAPTER FIVE

Specific Proposals for Market Reform in 1994

Market-oriented reform of our health care system would be far better for the American people than ClintonCare. A case has been made for policies that would move us in the direction of a competitive, more efficient and fairer health care system. But to defeat Clinton's bureaucratic monster, we must avoid "moderate" compromises suggested by Senator Chafee (R. Rhode Island) and others, who would allow the Clintons to achieve their goal of much more bureaucracy and a vastly larger welfare state. Radical legislative surgery to deal with the system's problems is unnecessary.

William Kristol, chairman of the Project for the Republican Future, has set the gauntlet: "Opponents of the Clinton health plan should immediately propose simple federal legislation that fixes the most serious problems in American health care—and force the president to explain why he says no to it."[61] The following proposals are realistic and doable alternatives that treat real problems but without the irreversible damage. Haste makes waste, especially when considering the monumental enlargement of government in our lives that would be the inevitable outcome of Clinton's bureaucratic plan.

Radical legislative surgery to deal with the system's problems is unnecessary.

And, as Senator Daniel Patrick Moynihan and many others would hope, an exhausting confrontation over the health care system's fifteen percent of the economy could be avoided so that the President's important and unfilled promise of welfare reform might receive the priority that it deserves. If the Congress were to limit its attention to the following five proposals in 1994, then time and energy would permit important welfare and crime legislation to also be realized in 1994.

(1) Congress should amend the tax code that currently gives health insurance subsidies only to those who receive their health care coverage through their employer. Health insurance premiums should be made fully deductible for everyone. This would lower insurance costs for the self-employed and, in particular, those working for firms that do not provide health insurance benefits to their employees. This is doable in 1994.

(2) Congress should expand the portability of health insurance and reduce the anxiety about health care security when changing or losing one's job by amending the existing COBRA legislation. Individuals and families need to have expanded options to take their health insurance with them when leaving an employer. This is doable in 1994.

(3) Congress should eliminate legislative and regulatory barriers that restrict the ability of small-businesses to voluntarily form insurance pools in order to collectively negotiate with large health care providers. This would give small businesses bargaining

power, which is the important benefit to be gained through managed competition. But this kind of reform would *not* be a lightening rod for a new National Health Board and all the government purchasing alliances and other bureaucracies that would result from the Clinton plan. This is doable in 1994.

(4) Congress should authorize medisave accounts that are not subject to the "use it or lose it" requirement, as is currently required of "flexible spending accounts" that are permitted by the IRS. Goodman and Musgrave have proposed a revenue-neutral plan—to avoid lower federal revenues during the current period of fiscal restraint—in which employers and employees would be permitted to deposit in medisave accounts untaxed premium savings from changes to higher deductible, catastrophic policies.[62] This proposal would encourage greater vigilance by consumers regarding their health care spending decisions and begin to generate the benefits described earlier in the previous chapter. This is doable in 1994.

As Senator Daniel Patrick Moynihan hopes, an exhausting confrontation over the health care system's fifteen percent of the economy could be avoided so that the President's important and unfilled promise of welfare reform might receive the priority that it deserves.

(5) Congress should consider legislation that would authorize and fund tax credits or vouchers for low-income families in order to increase the affordability of health insurance. Many working Americans, who are not eligible for Medicaid, would be assisted. If approved this would be a first installment on the eventual elimination of Medicaid and the empowerment of

individuals and families. This is doable in 1994.

There are a number of other specific actions that should be considered. But these five proposals would move us significantly in the direction of a health care system in which the consumer would once again be sovereign, market solutions encouraged, and more competition brought to health care markets. And, importantly, Americans would remain free of the massive new bureaucracies which would require that we sacrifice our freedoms, but which would also fail to solve the problem of escalating health care costs.

President Clinton and Hillary Rodham Clinton must have their feet held to the fire to explain to the American people why a focused and limited approach to change is inferior to their centralized and bureaucratic, that is, socialist scheme!

President Clinton and Hillary Rodham Clinton must have their feet held to the fire to explain to the American people why a focused and limited approach to change is inferior to their centralized and bureaucratic, that is, socialist scheme.

Government's high-cost involvement in health care is indeed a crisis. But the solution is certainly not to turn the existing private system over to the bureaucrats. The administration knows it. Radical reform is not necessary. The administration knows it. Health care quality has suffered in all bureaucratic, nationalized health care systems. The administration knows it. The rate of increase in health care costs in nationalized systems has been equal or greater than ours in recent years. The administration knows it. Apparently, most important of all, political success in majoritarian democracies seems to require that those in power give "free" goodies to the middle class, and not just to the very poor. Unfortunately, the Clintons seem to know this as well.

CHAPTER SIX

Conclusion

The social engineers in the Clinton administration are hard at work trying to politicize and control health care in America. But the issue is bigger than just health care. Our future as a relatively free society will be determined by which of two competing visions of social arrangements triumphs in this debate over America's health care system.

Our future as a relatively free society will be determined by which of two competing visions of social arrangements triumphs in this debate over America's health care system.

One vision, derived from the wisdom of the Founding Fathers, fears centralized political power and therefore favors decentralized and, wherever possible, private and voluntary solutions to social and economic problems. In this vision, the world would be full of free and sovereign individuals possessing inalienable rights to life, liberty and the pursuit of happiness.

And notice the crucial distinction: "rights" are about possibilities, not about guarantees; we are free to pursue happiness. It is a wholly different issue whether individual A has a "right," enforced by government, to the money of individual B in order to achieve A's purposes.[63]

The general question of "rights, and therefore our current preoccupation with "entitlements" to "universal coverage," deserves to be debated again as it was in the eighteenth century by the founding fathers who were responsible for the American Declaration of Independence.

The history of non-free societies, such as the former Soviet Union or the Peoples' Republic of Korea, shows that freedom is possible only if based on private ownership, free, competitive markets, and limited government.

Measured in terms of President Clinton's cabinet appointments and the direction the administration's "covenant for change" has taken, the Clintons appear to prefer the latter vision of political bureaucracy and command and control.

The other vision, a much older vision, is all about political power, regimentation, and tyrants. Whether of the "left" in Stalin's Soviet Union and Mao's People's Republic of China, or of the "right" in Mussolini's Fascist Italy or the horror of Hitler's experimentation with National Socialism, command and control steers these tyrannical social systems. Rule is by force. Individuals serve the ends of the almighty state, and citizens' lives are paternalistically controlled in the same manner that parents watch over their small children. It is a vision that sets employers against employees, big companies against small ones, doctors against patients, and the old against the young. Market solutions are peaceful solutions. Politicized solutions pit one group against another and always become antagonistic.

Measured in terms of President Clinton's cabinet appointments and the direction the administration's "covenant for change" has taken, the Clintons appear to prefer the latter vision of political bureaucracy and command and control. And ironically, this lurch to the left reappears in the U. S. as the rest of the world searches for ways to move toward voluntary social arrangements and limits to the role of government in human affairs.

The Clinton plan would establish at least four new layers of government bureaucracy between patients and their elected representatives, not to mention the implied interference in the patient-doctor relationship.

ClintonCare is the largest political power grab this country has ever known. As noted earlier, the Health Security Act would, for starters, create at least 59 new federal programs or bureaucracies, expand 20 others, and impose 79 new federal mandates. Far and away the largest tax increase ever would be disguised, they hope, as an employer mandate. The Clinton plan would establish at least four new layers of government bureaucracy between patients and their elected representatives, not to mention the implied interference in the patient-doctor relationship.

As history invariably shows—witness our experience with Medicare, Medicaid, and Veterans' Administration programs—the feared growth of bureaucracy with the creation of new government programs turns out to be far larger than even the critics had predicted at the outset. The rapid growth in the U.S. Department of Education, the Department of Energy, and the Department of Health and Human Services, for example, also makes the point. Humorist Dave Barry, looking back over 1993 at the new year, captured the essence of the problem: "In a major address, President Clinton announces that the nation's current health care system is bloated, inefficient, unresponsive, overpriced, wasteful and stupid, and that therefore he wants to turn control of it over to: the federal government"[64]

Recently, on a visit to the United States, Wilfred Prewo, chief executive of the Chamber of Industry and Commerce in Hanover, Germany, observed how similar the Clinton plan would be to the current German health care system—health alliances and employer-mandated payroll taxes for example. In a speech to the National Governor's Association, however, the message was worrisome. The German system is experiencing severe financial strain and the health alliances have become little governments all to themselves.[65]

The health care reform plan of President Clinton and Hillary Rodham Clinton would run counter to the principles that have made America work so well.

More importantly, in terms of Senator Moynihan's "fantasy" remark on financing the Clinton plan, the average German payroll tax rate needed to finance health spending equal to 10.6 percent of GDP, is now 13.4 percent. Compare this with Clinton's assertion that a 10 or 11 percent payroll tax in the U.S. (7.9 percent on employers and the other 20 percent of the total paid by employees) would finance health care spending in the U.S. which is already 14 percent of GDP and will, by the Clinton administration's own admission, rise to more than 17 percent of GDP by the end of the decade.

It is sometimes difficult to know whether the Clinton program is being driven by a misguided faith in central planning, arrogance, moral outrage, socialist ideology, or other unknown motives.   But good intentions and intellectual merit are irrelevant. The health care reform plan of President Clinton and Hillary Rodham Clinton would run counter to the principles that have made America work so well compared to known alternatives.

ClintonCare is not about reform, and it doesn't solve a crisis. It is a Great Leap Forward into health care socialism from which it would be difficult to withdraw.

The Clinton vision, drawing on the older model of power and control, confuses, nay contradicts, what the founding fathers meant by "rights."   It mandates burdens on some for the benefit of others whose personal conduct lacks the discipline that comes from personal responsibility. With its forced transfers of wealth and loss of freedom for health care consumers and providers, it would be the most destructive policy to

All Americans want a health care system based on security, cost-efficiency, choice, and quality. ClintonCare is not that system and should be rejected.

our liberties ever. ClintonCare is not about reform, and it doesn't solve a crisis. It is a Great Leap Forward into health care socialism from which it would be difficult to withdraw. In short, all Americans want a health care system based on security, cost-efficiency, choice, and quality. But ClintonCare is not that system and should be rejected.

Notes

1. On Greenberg's 1991 strategy to recapture the White House see Stanley Greenberg, "From Crisis to Working Majority," *The American Prospect,* Fall 1991.

2. David Wessel and Gerald F. Seib, "Clinton Had Devised His Health Package Before the Inaugural," *The Wall Street Journal,* September 22, 1993.

3. Ibid.

4. P. J. O'Rourke, "Health Reform: License to Kill," *The Wall Street Journal,* September 23, 1993.

5. Merrill Mathews and Molly Hering, "The Clinton Plan," Second Opinions: Health Care Supplement, *National Review,* December 1993, p. 10.

6. Charley Reese, "How Bureaucracies Are Born," *Conservative Chronicle,* December 6, 1993.

7. See for example the chart by Congressman Richard Armey (R, Texas) that attempts to show the bureaucratic relationships that would exist under the Clinton plan in "Your Future Health Plan," *The Wall Street Journal,* October 13, 1993.

8. David B. Rivkin, Jr., "Health Care Reform V. the Founders," *The Wall Street Journal,* September 29, 1993. Also see Joseph Sobran, "Government's Appetite for

Power Is Boundless," *Conservative Chronicle,* August 25, 1993; Murray Rothbard, "The Clinton Health Plan: The Devil's in the Principles," *Essays in Political Economy,* Ludwig von Mises Institute, No. 17, October 1993; and Robert J. Barro, "The New Socialism," *The Wall Street Journal,* October 25, 1993.

9.   Alain Enthoven, "A Good Health Care Idea Gone Bad," *The Wall Street Journal,* October 7, 1993.

10. Quoted in Peter Samuel, "Health Care Reform Politics," *National Review,* May 24, 1993, p. 35

11. See Thomas J. DiLorenzo, "Clinton Health Plan Salutes Italy's Past," *The Wall Street Journal,* October 26, 1993 for the comparison between Italy's disastrous experimentation with Fascism and Clinton's health care reform plan.

12. Marianne M. Jennings, "A Mother Talks to Mrs. Clinton," *The Wall Street Journal,* January 3, 1994. The article also appeared as "Hillary Should Try Threading Health Care Maze," *The Arizona Republic,* January 9, 1994.

13. See John C. Goodman and Gerald L. Musgrave, *Patient Power: Solving America's Health Care Crisis,* (CATO Institute: Washington, D.C.), 1992, Chapters 7 and 10.

14. Ibid., Chapter 10 - Increasing Government Control Over the Price and Quality of Medical Care.

15. Aneurin Bevan, *In Place of Fear,* (Heinemann: London), 1952, p. 76.

16. John C. Goodman and Gerald L. Musgrave, *Twenty Myths About National Health Insurance,* National Center for Policy Analysis, Dallas, Texas, NCPA Policy Report No. 166, December 1991, pp. 22-27.

17. Kazanjian, Arminee, et. al., *Fee Practice Medical Expenditures Per Capita and Full-Time Equivalent Physicians in British Columbia, 1987-1988,* (University of British Columbia: Vancouver), 1989, pp. 121-176.

18. From Enoch Powell, *Medicine and Politics,* 1975 cited in Goodman and Musgrave, *Twenty Myths,* p. 66.

19. Goodman and Musgrave, *Twenty Myths,* p. 27.

20. Quoted in Merrill Mathews and Molly Hering, "The Clinton Plan," p. 10.

21. See, for example, the insightful editorial "The Health Care Debate," *The Wall Street Journal,* September 22, 1993.

22. Paul Starr speech "Where Do We Go From Here?," before the American Pharmaceutical Association, Honolulu, Hawaii, November 15, 1993.

23. Edward R. Annis, M.D., "Second Opinions: American Health Care Today," Health Care Supplement, *National Review,* December 1993, p. 2.

24. See for example E. Emmett Tyrrell, Jr. *Conservative Chronicle,* November 17, 1993 and Elizabeth McCaughey, *The Wall Street Journal,* November 22, 1993 for examinations of these issues.

25. Thomas Sowell, *Conservative Chronicle,* November 17, 1993.

26. Goodman and Musgrave, *Patient Power,* p. 77.

27. See the discussion in Goodman and Musgrave, *Twenty Myths,* pp. 76-78.

28. Cited in Peter Samuel, *National Review,* May 24, 1993, p. 37.

29. Jeremy Rosner of the Progressive Policy Institute, the research arm of the Democratic Leadership Council, "A Progressive Plan for Affordable, Universal Health Care," in Will Marshall and Martin Schram, eds., *Mandate for Change,* (Berkley Books: New York), 1993, pp. 107-128.

30. *Health Care Update: The Need for Health Care Reform,* August 1993, pp. 23-24.

31. Ibid., p. 38.

32. The quotation from Clinton's Health Security Act draws on the detailed examination of all 1,342 pages by

Elizabeth McCaughey of the Manhattan Institute. See "Price Controls on Health Care," *The Wall Street Journal,* November 22, 1993 for the page references.

33. Bill Clinton, "Putting People First: A National Economic Strategy for America," in Robert E. Levin, *Bill Clinton: The Inside Story,* (Shapolsky Publishers, Inc.: New York), 1992. Also see Peter Samuel, "Health-Reform Politics," *National Review,* May 24, 1993.

34. Quoted in Elizabeth McCaughey, "Price Controls on Health Care."

35. J. D. Kleinke, "The Health Care Inflation Fantasy," *The Wall Street Journal,* October 18,1993.

36. See e.g. John C. Goodman and Gerald L. Musgrave, *Twenty Myths.*

37. Reference to Mitchell Senate bill in Rush Limbaugh, *See I Told You So,* (Simon & Schuster, Inc.: New York), 1993, p. 157. Also see Goodman and Musgrave, *Patient Power,* pp. x-xi.

38. See Paul Greenberg, *Conservative Chronicle,* November 17, 1993, p. 5.

39. See e.g. Hedrick Smith, *The Russians,* (The New York Times Book Co.: New York), First Revised Edition, December 1984, Chapter I. - The Privileged Class: Dachas and Zils.

40. This and the following discussion has especially used Carlos Bonilla, "The Price of a Health Care Mandate," *The Wall Street Journal,* August 20, 1993; Martin Feldstein, "The Health Plan's Financing Gap," *The Wall Street Journal,* September 29, 1993; and Linda Gorman, "Colorado Care: Is the Cure Worse Than the Disease?," *Independence Issue Paper,* Independence Institute, Denver, Colorado, October 25, 1993. Bonilla is the chief economist of the Employment Policies Institute and Feldstein is a Harvard economist and former Chairman of the President's Council of Economic Advisers.

41. See Martin Feldstein, "Clinton's Hidden Health Tax," *The Wall Street Journal,* November 10, 1993; Paul G. Merski, "Hiding a Tax, Off Budget," *The Wall Street*

Journal, December 3, 1993; and Paul Craig Roberts, "Clinton's Health Care Plan Is a Socialist Plot."

42. Feldstein, "Clinton's Hidden Health Tax."

43. John C. Goodman and Gerald L. Musgrave, *Patient Power,* pp. 29-30. This book is essential reading if one is to understand how we came to have the health care system that we have and the changes required to achieve a more efficient and responsive system. A much shorter introduction is Gary Robbins, Aldona Robbins and John C. Goodman, *How Our Health System Works,* National Center for Policy Analysis, Dallas, Texas, NCPA Policy Report No. 177, February 1993. A shorter version of *Patient Power* is now available from the CATO Institute in Washington, D.C. An even briefer, highly readable version is Goodman's essay, "Health Insurance," in David R. Henderson, ed., *The Fortune Encyclopedia of Economics,* (Warner Books, Inc: New York), 1993.

44. Thomas Sowell, "You Will Pay More for Less Under Hillary's Plan," *Conservative Chronicle,* September 29, 1993.

45. Goodman and Musgrave, *Patient Power,* p. 32.

46. David R. Stutz, Bernard Feder, and the editors of Consumer Reports Books, *The Savvy Patient: How to Be an Active Participant in Your Medical Care,* (Consumer Reports Books: Mount Vernon, New York), 1990.

47. Grace-Marie Arnett, "The Clinton Plan and Others," p. 34.

48. A number of examples of the wage value of subsidized benefits under the present federal tax code can be found in Goodman and Musgrave, *Patient Power,* pp. 263-268. The value of the benefit equals the formula $1/1-t$, where t is the sum of the marginal tax rates on the federal income tax, the FICA tax (including the "employer's" so-called contribution) and the state and local income tax. For example if $t = .28 + .153 + .06$ then $1/1-t$ equals $1/1-.493$ and $1/.507$ equals 1.97.

49. "The American system of *employer*-funded health insurance, whose distortions the government is now trying to cure, is the completely unintended consequence

of an earlier government edict: wage and price controls during World War II. Employers, unable to bid for labor with higher wages, bid with control-exempt health-benefit packages. Ever since, the federal tax system has built a protective wall around third-party payments." Peter Samuel, "Health Care Reform Politics," p. 35.

50. Cited in *Patient Power,* p. 43.

51. Federal COBRA law enables an individual to keep their employer-based medical insurance for up to 18 months if the individual pays the premiums. Of course, if you are out of work, that might be difficult. Personalized and portable health insurance can be facilitated by self-insurance through medisave accounts. See the discussion below.

52. Robbins, Robbins and Goodman, *How Our Health Care System Works,* p. 22.

53. Ibid., p. 23.

54. Goodman and Musgrave, *Patient Power,* p. 257.

55. See Goodman and Musgrave, *Twenty Myths,* pp. 36-37 and Goodman and Musgrave, *Patient Power,* pp. 253-257.

56. *Patient Power,* pp. 31-32 and pp. 598-605.

57. "Now the Good News on Health Care," *The Wall Street Journal,* September 20, 1993.

58. See for example Rosalind Resnick, "Enlisting Employees in the Battle to Cut Health Care Cost," *Business and Health,* June 1993, pp. 24-29 and Chris Warden, "Letting Employees Rein in Costs: Firms Save on Health Care by Letting Market Work," *Investor's Business Daily,* May 20, 1993.

59. See the illustrative example in Goodman and Musgrave, *Patient Power,* on pp. 233-243, in particular Figure 8.3.

60. Goodman and Musgrave, *Patient Power,* pp. 63-65.

61. See William Kristol, "How to Oppose the Health Plan—And Why," *The Wall Street Journal,* January 11, 1994. For other examples of specific actions that would be

desirable and doable, see Goodman and Musgrave, *Patient Power,* p.649-657.

62. *Patient Power,* p. 247.

63. See the excellent discussion of the issue and meaning of "rights" in Michael J. Hurd, "Health Care in America: The Leading Edge of Mediocrity," *Atlantis,* vol. 1, No. 4, July 1993.

64. Dave Barry, "1993's Final Tally: President Bubba 1, Biosphere 2," *The Arizona Republic,* January 2, 1994.

65. Wilfried Prewo, "Germany is not a Model," *The Wall Street Journal*, February 1, 1994.

Suggested Reading

Bast, Joseph L., Rue, Richard C. and Wesbury, Stuart A., *Why We Spend Too Much on Health Care,* (The Heartland Institute: Chicago), 1992.

Goodman, John C. and Musgrave, Gerald L., *Patient Power: Solving America's Health Care Crisis,* (CATO Institute: Washington, D.C.), 1992.

Goodman, John C. and Musgrave, Gerald L., *Twenty Myths About National Health Insurance,* National Center for Policy Analysis, Dallas, Texas, NCPA Policy Report No. 166, December 1991.

Robbins, Gary, Robbins, Aldona, and Goodman, John C., *How Our Health System Works,* National Center for Policy Analysis, Dallas, Texas, NCPA Policy Report No. 177, February 1993.

Wasley, Terree P., *What Has Government Done to Our Health Care,* (CATO Institute: Washington, D.C.), 1992.

About the Author

A Senior Economist at the prestigious National Center for Policy Analysis, Barry Asmus writes, testifies and speaks on political and business issues facing America. Widely recognized for his views on making the U.S. a world-class competitor through total quality management and market incentives, Dr. Asmus has twice been voted the Outstanding Professor of the Year as well as receiving the Freedom Foundation at Valley Forge Award for Private Enterprise Education. His weekly commentary can be heard in Los Angeles on radio station KMNY. His other books include: *Crossroads: The Great American Experiment; The Space Place; and Supermyths: An Almanac of Political Fables.*

Forsooth, Forsooth

Forsooth, forsooth,
I lost a tooth
In a stick of gum one day.
Forsooth, forsooth,
Without my tooth
What would the Clinton's say?

Oh! From a White House tower
This problem is no puzzle.
Their answer here was crystal clear,
"Gum chewers need a muzzle!"

Then folks replied
From Wrigley's side
"Gum chewing," they asserted,
"Is such an old established right,
It musn't be deserted."

But in the halls of Congress
Special interests held no sway.
Health Care laws were drafted
And mouthbelts saved the day.

And so, throughout this land of ours,
Where health care laws are made,
All teeth are cleaned by government
Only freedom has decayed.

–Barry Asmus

What Can You Do?

ClintonCare is not about reform, and it doesn't solve a crisis. It is a Great Leap Forward into health care socialism from which it would be difficult to withdraw. Unfortunately, the Cooper plan isn't the answer either. Neither is the Chaffee plan or Senator Wellstone's single-payer system. The real problems in our health care system, the absence of market competition and empowered consumers, are not addressed by these plans. They would simply add more layers of government bureaucracy rather than move toward the market solutions proposed in this book. Please write or call to order copies for friends, colleagues and your elected representatives. You can make a difference!

CLINTONCARE:
Putting Government in Charge of Your Health by Dr. Barry Asmus

Published by *AMERIPRESS*
3420 East Shea Blvd., Suite 235
Phoenix, AZ 85028
(602) 953-5149

Yes! Please send *CLINTONCARE* to:

Name:_____

Company:_____

Address:_____

City:_____ State:_____Zip:_____

_____Single copy @ $9.95 plus $2.00 S&H .... $_____

_____2-10 copies @ $7.95 plus $1.00 S&H each ....: .... $_____

_____40% discount on larger orders plus 50¢ S&H each

or call (602)953-5149 for information .... $_____

Arizona residents add 6.8% sales tax .... $_____

TOTAL ENCLOSED .... $_____

Make your check or money order payable to AmeriPress and send to:
3420 E. Shea Blvd. #235, Phoenix, AZ 85028.